M000218532

CARLOS "MASTER" MUÑOZ

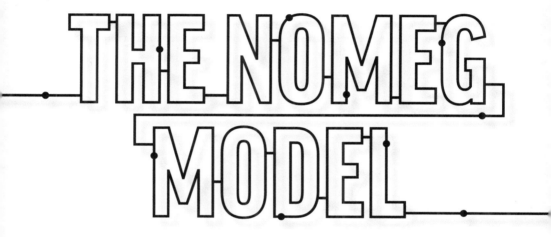

THE NOMEG MODEL

CREATING A PROFITABLE INTERNATIONAL COMPANY WITHOUT MONEY FROM INVESTORS

Published by Advantage, Charleston, South Carolina.
Member of Advantage Media Group.

ADVANTAGE is a registered trademark, and the Advantage colophon is a trademark of Advantage Media Group, Inc.

Printed in the United States of America.

10 9 8 7 6 5 4 3 2 1

ISBN: 978-1-64225-174-6
LCCN: 2021922058

Cover design by David Taylor.
Layout design by Wesley Strickland.

This publication is designed to provide accurate and authoritative information in regard to the subject matter covered. It is sold with the understanding that the publisher is not engaged in rendering legal, accounting, or other professional services. If legal advice or other expert assistance is required, the services of a competent professional person should be sought.

Advantage Media Group is proud to be a part of the Tree Neutral® program. Tree Neutral offsets the number of trees consumed in the production and printing of this book by taking proactive steps such as planting trees in direct proportion to the number of trees used to print books. To learn more about Tree Neutral, please visit **www.treeneutral.com**.

Advantage Media Group is a publisher of business, self-improvement, and professional development books and online learning. We help entrepreneurs, business leaders, and professionals share their Stories, Passion, and Knowledge to help others Learn & Grow. Do you have a manuscript or book idea that you would like us to consider for publishing? Please visit **advantagefamily.com**.

To Marisela, Helio, Miia, and Mayer.

CONTENTS

INTRODUCTION

It all began with a Monday. Not just any Monday, though. I remember the day, in part, because I attended a wedding the night before. (Who gets married on a Sunday, by the way?) I returned to the office the next morning still reeling from my hangover. I walked through the large open room of workstations to my office along the back wall, a glass-encased room with a door I normally kept open only when I was there. On this morning, however, I found three twentysomethings cramped around my desk working on their laptops plastered with stickers. At first, I thought I had entered the wrong office, maybe an intern hub of some sort. I took two steps backward and checked that it was my name on the door. It was.

"What's going on?" I asked, confusion and a bit of loftiness slowing down my thoughts and voice.

I panned around the room looking at the photographs, books, and furniture, trying again to confirm that I hadn't entered the wrong office. I hadn't.

"Why are all of you in my office?" I wasn't angry, just bewildered.

"Bro, didn't you get the email from HR?" one of them asked.

"Bro? No. Who reads the emails from HR? That's like birthday spam."

"Well, you should read this one," another of them said.

I turned and went straight to the HR manager's desk, asking her to pull up the email she had sent to the team. She stopped what she was doing immediately, not because I made her but perhaps from concern for my contorted face. The email was actually a cost analysis conducted by one of my business unit leaders, detailing the numbers from a project testing out a new business idea. I asked her to scroll down and get to the part where my office was involved. The project had received immediate traction and begun generating more revenue for the company. As a result, it needed more people behind it to continue its growth. The leader put together a team to continue with the idea and analyzed the costs of renting a new office for the team to use. There it was! A segment of the report analyzed the amount of time I was spending in my office. They did a separate analysis examining the last three months and found that I had only spent about eight hours behind my desk each month. Those bastards.

They crossed the analyses and said, "Carlos was never in his office the last three months. We need offices. Let's use his office." As I was reading the email, I began to feel a burning anger building inside me. My mind started spinning. I struggled to link my thoughts together as the sorts of mental barriers I so often advise people to avoid began to take hold.

I knew I needed to cool off before I said anything that I may later regret, so I took a walk and then attended a few meetings. Several hours had passed when a realization became clear to me: losing my office was perhaps the most important thing that had happened to me over my fifteen-year entrepreneurial career. It was finally happening. The organization was trying new ideas without me. Their needs had shifted, and they were making decisions to accommodate those changes without the need for authorization.

Very few companies can actually throw an owner out of their own office, and even fewer can do it knowing that the owner will respect that decision on the basis that it's what's best for the company. Whether we like it or not, in many ways we still live in a hierarchical society, one in which a relatively small number of people control a majority of buying power, media influence, political and legislative sway, and access to large sums of financial capital. This book is the manual for building a company capable of overriding that system and leveling the playing field, so to speak, of an often unfair game.

Before we go any further, let me introduce myself. I am a living, breathing new breed of entrepreneur. I constantly challenge the status quo and have been doing it since I was a kid, not out of plain rebelliousness, but because of the way I see the world. I founded this company that just threw me out of my office. I started that multimillion-dollar company from scratch and grew it—without any capital from outside investors—to having offices in twenty countries, a staff of more than three hundred employees, and the best part: it runs without me. Those three sentences took approximately fifteen years to turn into a reality. Those fifteen years were complicated. I almost went bankrupt twice. I worked much more than I should have and came very close to burning out more times than I can count.

I started creating content using the company's blog, and after two years of talking to an empty theater, little by little I grew a following within the real estate community. As I was growing my company, I was also building a persona, cultivating an audience, and broadening my content: sales, entrepreneurship, finances, technology, social media, and anything else that could help even out the odds against individual and small business success in a capital-strapped reality. I learned to stand out and build a personal brand, and suddenly, that blog grew to what I now call a social media empire and a tribe of more than one million entrepreneurs. I talk about business the same way I talk about life. For me, they're intertwined. Those fifteen years of building my companies and my personal brand were my real business school. They showed me that what you've read about business in the past will *not* get you through the grind of building a business today.

Virtually everything I learned in school about entrepreneurship and building a large company turned out to be bullshit, and I'm willing to bet that you've had your head filled with the same useless nonsense too. That may be why you're here reading my book, or maybe you're one of the lucky ones who hasn't endured a stream of academics and corporate executives regurgitating business school theories into your ears. Whatever the case, I'm glad that you're here seeking out new ideas. I spent years learning all that garbage and nearly lost everything applying it before I built a model that actually works for capital-deprived entrepreneurs regardless of the industry or geographic location.

After exiting my first company (a property development and consulting firm), I created two more companies: a real estate fund and the social media empire I just mentioned. I've achieved immediate results by implementing what you're about to learn in this book.

It is possible to grow an international, multimillion-dollar company without outside investors.

Let me be clear: it is possible to grow an international, multimillion-dollar company without outside investors, whether the company be in the digital and technology space, the real estate development industry, or even a brick-and-mortar business. Regardless of the industry, it is possible for any company to run without its founder or CEO.

This is the book that challenges all assumptions. This is the book that venture capitalists don't want you to read. The ugly truth of the matter is that they have been lying to you in hopes of keeping entrepreneurs and the real creators from excluding venture capital from their companies. They want you to believe that you need them, that you cannot build and grow a company exponentially without their deep pockets. They are wrong, and they want you to be wrong too! This is the book that can and will change your life. And it is all built upon a specific and new business model: *the neural organization.*

This is the book that can and will change your life.

But let's go back to the beginning. If you draw a line from the beginning to the end of my model's development, it took me roughly fifteen years to find the working solutions I desired. That's fifteen years from the day that I started walking the walk as an entrepreneur until the day I stepped out of my first company, 4S Real Estate. Today my companies work without me. In essence, this is a story about those fifteen years and how they revealed to me the ways in which I could create a better business machine. Thanks to those fifteen years, I was able to reach results much faster in my new companies than my previous one, mainly because I already knew the way. My primary goal with this book is to ensure that you have the tools to do the same thing. I don't want you to get to the same point after twenty years of trying; I want you to do it *fast*, and I want you to do it without having to give away all your financial security and/or controlling power just to build a successful business on your own.

You don't have to look very hard to discover scary statistics on entrepreneurship in the US: Approximately 95 percent of businesses die within their first five years. About a quarter of those fail within their first year. Some 75 percent of all venture capital–backed start-ups fail. The 5 percent that do survive eventually stop growing. The list goes on and on. These businesses either build themselves upon the foundation of an outdated organizational model, keep incompetent management in the driver's seat, grow too quickly with expensive capital, don't grow at all, or commit some combination of these poor choices. Either way, they're screwed in the end.

You'll hear a lot of academics, consultants, and other business thought leaders attribute these statistics to the times we're living in; and indeed, the times in which we're currently living are incredibly VUCA: volatile, uncertain, complex, and ambiguous. But writing off our business failures as a function of the era isn't actually *helpful*, no matter how comforting an excuse it may be. Statistics such as these seem intent on assuring us that we will fail as entrepreneurs, while much of the literature pushes us in the other direction: *try, go for it, just do it.* To make matters worse, just saying that they are simply a sign of the times does nothing to help keep our businesses, and the ones we wish to create, alive.

Aspiring entrepreneurs need to start acting on their business ideas right now. They can't afford to wait for politics and economies to stabilize, because it's unlikely that they ever will for any significant length of time. Leaders of existing large companies can't press pause on their businesses, either. They need to find a way to establish resilience and keep growing *today*.

Of course, I'm not the first person to notice this problem. There is plenty of literature out there that investigates how we can create growth and resilience during difficult times. When I was first starting out, I turned to those books for help. And for a long time, I believed in them. But I wasn't finding success. Eventually, I realized that it was because they didn't speak to the challenges that I was facing.

Business literature is usually targeted at large companies, or better, it deals with the idea of creating and growing a business that will be larger than life. It's largely comprised of books that present what I call "Big to Bigger" concepts. They can give you a sense of what happens in the corporate world, but they are far from being a practical tool for one person starting a company on their own. I'm willing to bet that either you or people around you know the methods applied in huge corporations. Pundits and industry insiders speak ad nauseum about their efficiency, how they manage global teams, how they move money around in such sophisticated and complex ways that you couldn't possibly understand them. You may even imagine that one day you'll be the CEO of a multinational company and following the ways of "the big boys" is how you'll do it. I still see interns with business books that were popular in the seventies and eighties, books that their college professors hold so sacred that, whether out of laziness or a lack of creativity, they pass on to them.

Now, you could argue that recently there has been a lot of start-up literature that can help aspiring entrepreneurs. The problem is that these books are centered on securing large amounts of start-up capital. They assume that all of us live in an ecosystem identical to the US, where capital is plentiful and all you need are the tools to secure it. Silicon Valley, in particular, hails a model that values growth over profit, using millions in venture capital to prop companies up in hopes that a big idea will land even bigger profits in time. That model also assumes that start-ups actually want investors in their company, who inevitably end up reaping most of the profits if the company is a hit one day.

Although I have companies in the US, I started in Latin American markets, where capital is scarce. None of the approaches I've read about, to date, could speak to the challenges that lay before me in Latin America. Of course, there were some ideas that I found helpful. If you know the work of authors like Eric Ries and Simon Sinek, for example, then you'll recognize some of their ideas in this book. But, ultimately, I learned that I would have to develop my own approach to entrepreneurship and business modeling if I wanted to succeed—so I did.

The **Neural Organization Model for Exponential Growth (NOMEG)** reinvents how companies are structured and reimagines what they can achieve. It's a model that prioritizes growth *and* profitability equally. It emphasizes the importance of innovation, experimentation, and collaboration. It rejects the notion of specialization in favor of a more nimble, adaptable approach that sidesteps competition and reduces our reliance on venture capital. I've used this system to build several of my own companies, which are now operating in nearly twenty regions across the globe. I've also used this model to help existing companies reinvent themselves, both in the US and in Latin America. And I've shared it with more than two hundred entrepreneurs who worked through my Mastermind program.

If anything has changed in the years since I got my start, it's that the world is even more VUCA than it used to be. A series of dramatic economic downturns have demonstrated that capital will not always be abundant, even in the US. There are so many regions and industries, both in the US and around the world, in which young entrepreneurs and veteran business leaders are looking for a low-capital approach to build, grow, and sustain their organizations. There are more people building their own brands today, thanks in large part to social media making so many ideas, data, and other useful bits of information available to everyone. As a result, the dialogue between and within tribes exploded. The bottom line is that a company's chances of going global, of growing exponentially and finding long-term success in multiple markets and industries, are much better in this kind of fast-moving, highly interconnected environment than they have ever been. That is precisely where my model thrives: in the future.

The NOMEG model is a combination of tools that applies to nine different areas of building a business. This model assumes that you already know the basics of starting a company but gives you the hacks you need to shorten your way to success and sustain it. The pyramid on the next page shows the different categories for which you will be learning specific business tools in this book. Each chapter correlates with a specific category, which will be indicated by a graphic at the beginning of each chapter.

In the ensuing chapters, I will explain how the neural organization model can transform the future of business, making success accessible to everyone—not just to those who have venture capital in short reach.

This book serves as a manual to the NOMEG model. Throughout the ensuing chapters, we're going to build the complete model based on the pyramid above by exploring exactly *how* and *why* the neural organization model works. Learning about each of the pyramid's concepts will enable you to build and implement the model's structure in your own business, whether you are a current business owner or aspiring to create one in the future. Every chapter coincides with a specific category in the pyramid, so by the end of the book, you will have a complete understanding of the NOMEG model from top to bottom.

In chapter zero and chapter 1, we'll discuss the biggest, most fundamental shift in the way that neural companies operate: via a network of business units. Chapter 2 demonstrates that in order for this model to succeed, companies need to prioritize teams over bosses. Given this new emphasis on teamwork, chapter 3 will reimagine the role of the CEO. Once we have a new understanding of what CEOs do, we'll also need a new understanding of what COOs and boards of directors do, which is what chapters 4 and 5 will provide.

After you understand the fundamental principles that drive neural businesses, we'll look at *why* businesses and entrepreneurs around the world are adopting this model. Chapter 6 offers a demonstration on how the neural model facilitates and expedites global expansion, while chapter 7 illustrates how it creates corporate resilience, protecting businesses and owners in volatile times. Chapter 8 explores the effect this approach has on company cultures, and then chapters 9 and 10 look at neural model success stories from around the world and across industries, and talk about finding that success for yourself.

By the end, you will have a full view of how the NOMEG model has the potential to transform our businesses, our jobs, and our economies. Ultimately, this book is a NOMEG owner's manual. Remember that any time you or your business stumbles or struggles to break through a wall, you can come back to this book and analyze which part of the model you're in and how to progress to the next level.

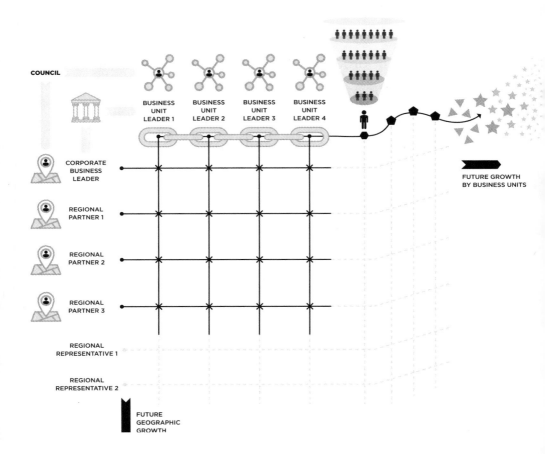

The book will help you understand the complete model as we reframe the future of business.

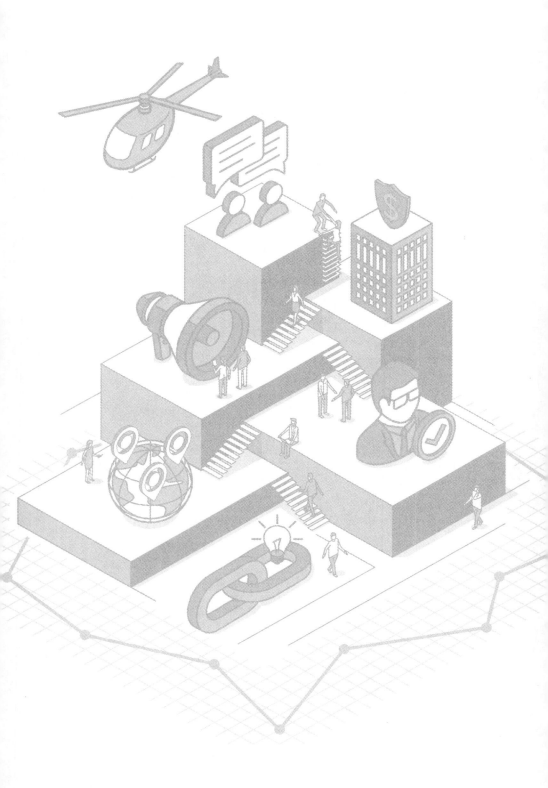

AN OVERVIEW OF THE NEURAL ORGANIZATION MODEL FOR EXPONENTIAL GROWTH (NOMEG)

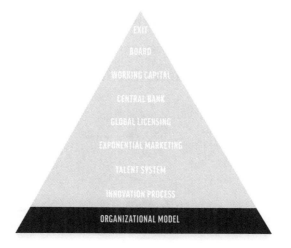

Let's start with a simple exercise. Imagine the organizational chart of a company. It can be your own company or the one you'd like to start.

Take out a piece of paper, and draw yourself; then draw every single position you think would be essential for your company's operation: think departments, think areas, think teams. Establish connections between everyone. How does it look?

Ninety-nine percent of the time that I propose this exercise, people come up with a traditional hierarchical model (see example below). Entrepreneurs and aspiring entrepreneurs alike rarely question what is really behind this model because it's so embedded in our minds (e.g., college is an absolute necessity, penny-saving, total dependency on investors, or any other outdated business belief system that we are still trying to deprogram from our instincts). It's amazing how you can even get the structure from clip art models off every presentation software used to date. Yes, people still use clip art from Microsoft Word.

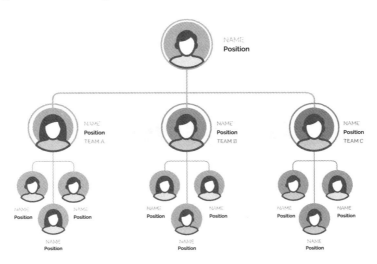

What you fail to understand is that this simple diagram dictates a lot of the culture inside a company. It limits people (they are always dependent on whoever sits above them) and the speed of innovation, ultimately diminishing the company's resilience. When we design organizations, the framework we use might be limiting their potential.

But why should you change a model that has been used for more than a hundred years? Because, quite simply, the world today crushes those organizations. You need to reframe businesses through a new model if you want them to thrive in the ever-changing future.

How did I stumble onto this new model? I "discovered" the model. The only reason I worked on changing my ideas was because the traditional ones did not work. The traditional hierarchical model failed me, as I was also guilty of following dated ideas about business and maybe even life itself. We'll get to some of those stories in later chapters.

WHAT IS THE NEURAL ORGANIZATION MODEL FOR EXPONENTIAL GROWTH?

A neural network consists of many interconnected neurons. In fact, it is a "simple" device that receives data at the input and provides a response. First, the neural network learns to correlate incoming and outcoming signals with each other—this is called "learning." Next, the neural network begins to work by receiving input data and generating output signals based on the accumulated knowledge.

The NOMEG system is an organizational structure in which independent "neurons" (made up of teams) collaborate with other "neurons" to create profitability and growth. The larger the network, the stronger the system becomes.

As we will see throughout the chapters of this book, the NOMEG system integrates

- both human and core system processes in one diagram,

- a democratic team culture,

- a holistic view of innovation and its integration with the talent structure,

- a sales strategy focused on aggressive global growth,

- a leader structure centered on accountability, and

- a clear purpose for the company's long-term view.

Before we dive into the specifics of the model, bear in mind that the NOMEG system is not based on a single idea. It's more akin to building a Swiss clock. Think of it. A Swiss clock is a beautiful piece of machinery when all the parts work together. When they do, you don't just get a clock; you get a piece of art that tells time.

I believe my companies are like that Swiss clock. They're not just companies that make money. They are a beautiful work of art, in that they are comprised of people working together to imagine, create, and operate a new future for the way we work. Organizational structures are often very cold and unemotional, but I will prove to you that creating work efficiencies and expanding a company can be a beautiful and profitable art form when using the NOMEG system.

NOMEG at Its Core

At its core, the NOMEG system is a matrix structure made up of two chains. We call those chains the **Edison Chain** and the **Napoleonic Chain**. Inside those chains there are "neurons," which represent the teams within a company that create and experiment with new business ideas. The foundational structure of this model asks us to redefine a company as a set of **business unit teams** and **business development teams**.

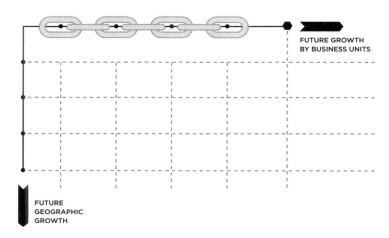

The business unit team is represented by the Edison Chain, and the business development team is represented by the Napoleonic Chain.

Remember, the NOMEG system was created for growing *profitable* companies, so the main structure is centered on the importance of cash flow. We will dive into how to manage this system financially in later chapters.

The business unit team is represented by the Edison Chain, and the business development team is represented by the Napoleonic Chain.

THE EDISON CHAIN

The American inventor and businessman Thomas Edison is regularly named among the greatest inventors of the modern era. During his lifetime, he accumulated a record 1,092 patents to his name (both singly and jointly). His devices contributed to electric power generation, mass communication, sound recording, and motion pictures, among other fields. The phonograph, the motion picture camera, and the long-lasting electric light bulb all exist due to the mind and determination of Edison. He was one of the first inventors to use organized science and research collaboration for the purposes of invention, often working in tandem with other inventors and scientific researchers, as well as his own employees. He even founded the first industrial research laboratory. He accomplished all this despite countless rejections and doubts from the world around him. An early teacher of his remarked that he was "too stupid to learn anything," and his first two employers fired him on grounds of being "nonproductive." He failed more than *ten thousand* times before the light bulb lit up and changed the face of civilization. But he never surrendered to the doubts, never gave up no matter how many setbacks or how much ridicule he endured.

He faced one of his biggest setbacks on December 10, 1914, when an explosion in West Orange, New Jersey, destroyed ten of his research buildings. No fewer than six fire crews tried in vain to extinguish the chemical blaze as Edison stood nearby and watched his life's work literally go up in smoke.

His son Charles walked over to his father and stood by him in stunned silence. As the story goes, Edison told him, "Charlie, go and get your mother and friends. They will never be able to see a spectacular fire like this in their entire life." Perhaps more stunned by his father's response than the fire itself, Charles asked him why he was not upset that everything he had built was being reduced to rubble. Edison reportedly replied, "Yes, our factory is being burnt down to ashes, but all the mistakes we have made are burnt down to ashes, too. We will start over again tomorrow."

I will say it bluntly: no multimillionaire entrepreneur has ever built their fortune on one business idea and one business idea alone.

Remove that lie from your head right now. Bill Gates and Steve Jobs made their billions by building businesses that reached many different market segments through a wide

No multimillionaire entrepreneur has ever built their fortune on one business idea and one business idea alone. array of tech-based products and services (e.g., computer software and hardware, telecommunications, internet technologies, apps, etc.). Jeff Bezos became the richest man on the planet not because he made a website to sell used books but because he created the infrastructure to gather together thousands of independent sellers of nearly any product in one virtual space. Even then, Amazon.com makes most of its revenue from business units that stand apart from its enormously popular retail website. Amazon Web Services, for instance, accounts for roughly 50 percent of Amazon.com's operating income by selling cloud computing services to individuals, companies, and governments around the world.

Now, more than ever, an entrepreneur's success hinges on their aptness for innovation and adaptability. New companies, no matter how small, must think like a major conglomerate. That's where my mind shifted to when I invented the Neural Organization Model for Exponential Growth (NOMEG). I had to find a way to reach as many different profit centers as I could, often relying on small profit margins from each unit to scale the company as a whole.

In a sense, any NOMEG company operates like an incubator/accelerator. NOMEG allows a company to create new business units continuously. I have strategy meetings every Monday with my teams in which we discuss new ideas and evaluate current and potential business units. All the leadership staff gives idea in these meetings. We will discuss how this process works in greater detail later on, but these collaborations are critical to NOMEG's success. The amount of innovation that goes on each week when you have dozens of people collaborating to find new ideas and refine existing business units is amazing. This is the Edison Chain in action.

The number of successful links a company owns at a certain point in time forms the Edison Chain. In chapter 1, I will explain in detail the innovation process used for creating these links.

Is it difficult work to do it this way? Yes and no. It takes many long days and nights to build the necessary infrastructure. It requires a lot of thought, research, and intuition when searching for the right ideas and people to incorporate into the company. But once you know how to find and empower bright, determined, entrepreneurial-minded people, new and profitable business units will form and run, to a certain extent, on their own. Does it take longer before you see major returns than, say, a Silicon Valley start-up that's fueled by $500 million in investments from disengaged but salivating venture capitalists? Yes. But the NOMEG model allows you to create a company that grows profit aggressively and controls operating risks while maximizing income for the founders without having to give away equity in the company.

The structure of a place with lots of access to capital like Silicon Valley is to emphasize growth over profit, at least initially. Once a large brand is created and takes over a market, then the profits come. The NOMEG model is designed to help businesses overcome capital shortages and generate stable profits in an aggressive way as they grow. Plus, all this can be done without the stress echoing from a chorus of outside opinions, demands, and complaints, to which you often are legally required to cater to.

Look at companies like Webvan and Theranos as examples. Both companies received hundreds of millions of dollars in capital from investors, yet both failed to make any money simply because their business model did not work. In Theranos's case, the technology they claimed to possess for taking and processing blood samples from an automated machine never actually existed. In the case of Webvan—a grocery delivery business formed in the midst of the dot-com bubble—the company tried to expand to cities all across the US without ever proving they could be profitable where they originated, a wealthy, booming, tech-craving San Francisco. They went bankrupt within three years of launching their brand.

Simply put, it is more feasible and controllable for you to build and scale a company by creating a diverse portfolio of related businesses that chain their profits to one another than it is to throw one business idea, Hail Mary–style, toward an invisible jackpot—all while carrying millions in debt on your back.

THE NAPOLEONIC CHAIN

The second chain that creates the NOMEG matrix is the Napoleonic Chain. It represents the geographic conquests of the organization.

I named it the Napoleonic Chain after the French emperor and military leader Napoleon, who was a master of geographic expansion and an ingenious tactician. Just take the Battle of Austerlitz (also known as the Battle of the Three Emperors) as an example. This battle is widely regarded among scholars as one of the most decisive engagements of the Napoleonic Wars and certainly one of Napoleon's greatest victories. Napoleon's *Grande Armée* of France defeated a much larger army made of combined Russian and Austrian forces led by Emperor Alexander I and Holy Roman Emperor Francis II.

Napoleon achieved what many experts argue was his greatest military victory of all by deliberately weakening his flank and faking a small defeat to lure the opposition into a disadvantaged position. When the enemy sent troops from its central ranks to engage the *Grande Armée*'s supposedly exposed flank, the French army attacked its weakened center, destroying it, and then tore through its flanks.

Napoleon's sweeping victory at the Battle of Austerlitz brought about the Treaty of Pressburg later in the month, which effectively ended the War of the Third Coalition. Today the battle is widely considered by scholars as a masterpiece in military tactics and leadership, allowing Napoleon and his allies to tighten their grip on territories in Central and Eastern Europe.

Like Napoleon, at the heart of the NOMEG system lies a willingness to grow geographically. Perhaps this is one of the most difficult parts I have to explain to entrepreneurs. Our minds are wired locally, and thus, thinking of a global expansion seems too complicated and/or unrealistic, especially for a start-up. I believed the same thing. But around 2011, we were facing challenging financial times, not because the company was doing poorly but because I'd made bad investment decisions outside the company. As a result, the money we were making out of Mexico was not enough to get us out of the problems we'd got ourselves into. I started traveling intensely during that time for speaking engagements. At first, one talk led to another, and while meeting new people in real estate, the idea to expand by giving them business units in their countries came to realization.

The growth across a large geographic landscape was truly quite simple. As I found the actual strategy to grow the Napoleonic chain without capital, I became aware that geographic growth is a capacity that very few companies achieve. This global mindset creates a proprietary distribution channel that most young companies fail to create. Once we dive into geographic growth, I will outline the specific tools that make this growth possible with no capital required. But for now, know that diversifying geographically is critical, especially in today's world in which markets are increasingly globally connected and technology makes it easier to exchange ideas, products, and services across the entire planet. Even as COVID-19 forced countries to close down their borders, technology still allows many businesses to continue operating in a "borderless" world. We get so many "stupid" businesses because an obscene number of entrepreneurs start companies with a locally wired mindset and vision. I like to call this phenomenon a two-block mentality, in that they think within a local radius, completely unaware of the possibilities of social media and the potential to grow more expansively, geographically. You must think bigger and broader.

The NOMEG Entrepreneur

Entrepreneurs today need to be both Edison and Napoleon. Like Edison, they must never stop innovating and experimenting, and like Napoleon, they must be smart and relentless in their quest to take new territory. The NOMEG model is, at its core, an organization in which **independent and autonomous teams** work together on both innovation (Edison Chain) and geographic penetration (Napoleon Chain). Both chains work together by channeling profit and responsibility through multiple **nodes**, representing the intersections where profit and responsibility meet.

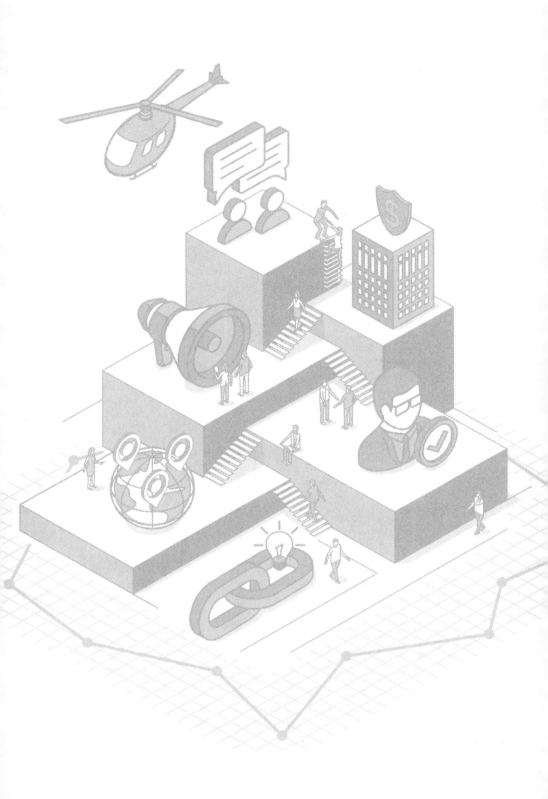

CHAPTER ONE

GETTING INNOVATION RIGHT

The Edison Chain

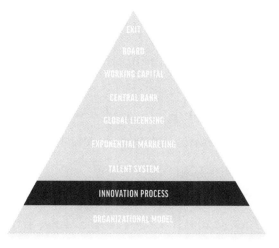

A few weeks before Christmas Day 2005, while sitting in an empty office, I told my business partner, Francisco, that we were finished. We had been working to build our company for a year and a half with little success, and by that December we had exhausted our credit lines and had no way to pay our mounting bills. We had given what cash we had left in our accounts to cover our staff's salaries, and my partner and I were contemplating whether we could raise enough cash by selling our office furniture—which we had bought inexpensively from another company following a flood—to pay the month's rent. Picture us in a small office that was once the starting point of two positive young entrepreneurs with hopes and dreams. We were all alone. Our employees had left the office a few hours ago, were probably Christmas shopping, and had absolutely no idea what was happening back in the workplace. If you drink, picture a half bottle of whiskey. It was late at night, and the future looked grim. It was a great setting for a sad Christmas movie.

"Do you have any credit left on your credit card?" I asked Francisco.

"Absolutely nothing," he said. "What about you?"

"All three of mine are completely full," I told him. "I could barely scrape together enough money to hop on a bus to visit my family, but it's Christmas, and I just can't miss it."

We stared at each other for a few seconds before Francisco closed his laptop and said, "Well, this is it. This is where it ends."

"What are we going to do about December's rent then?" I asked.

"Nothing," he said. Then he paused for a moment to scan the room. "If the landlord wants to charge us, tell him that he can keep the furniture or we can negotiate a deal once we come back in January. I tried to call him already, but he's on vacation."

"Well, we did what we could, partner," I said as I rose to my feet and patted him on the back. "Have a great vacation, and we can see each other here in January to clear out and lock up."

That was how my partner and I said good-bye at the end of 2005, just two years into the process of building a company together. Things didn't add up for me. That December was the end of a dream. We would have to begin looking for a traditional job. In that moment, I imagined myself waking up early—not by choice but because someone had set an artificial clock-in time for me—putting on a suit, maybe a boring tie, complying with whatever dress code my new employer had, packing my lunch in a plastic container, and driving in traffic for God-knows-how-many hours every day. We would just have to accept what the world tells us we're supposed to be: employees, employees forever. Nine-to-five, tie-wearing, traffic-prisoner employees.

I can still remember the sound of our laptops closing after trying to pay the last salary and seeing our account squarely at $0. Those who have experienced a moment like that know the excruciating pain and frustration of realizing that your company has made you lose everything.

I had two master's degrees and two undergraduate degrees, in economics and law respectively, yet there I was, on the verge of bankruptcy, considering selling old, water-damaged furniture to pay one month's rent for a penniless business. I was so frustrated with the fact that even though I had successfully completed everything that was asked of me in school, I couldn't complete the seemingly simple task of creating a sustainable business.

What had gone wrong? What was I missing? As it turned out, I, like many of you, had been misled into believing the false presumption that all you need for entrepreneurial prosperity is one great idea and a strong work ethic. Now that I look back, it sounds like a 1950s vision of the world, when there was enough wealth to get by with the basics. Maybe it was true at one point in time, perhaps in some far-off fantasyland where money rained down from every direction, but for me, in early 2000s Latin America, I was discovering quickly that nearly everything I had read and been taught about starting a business was a total lie.

Let's fast-forward a few years. That business with a $0 sum in the bank back in 2005 now has offices in eighteen countries, provides work for more than three hundred consultants and employees, and has won major contracts all over the world. I have gone on to write roughly a dozen books, earned dozens of international prizes for my work, and now dedicate most of my time to corporate education and investing in strategic assets through my investment platform. But all those accomplishments nearly never happened, had it not been for one phone call a few days into January 2006.

Fortunately for Francisco and me, just weeks after that god-awful Christmas of 2005, a client we had given a proposal to the previous summer called and told us he wanted to hire us for his project. We had forgotten all about that proposal, yet that was the deal that saved our business. You never know when your luck will turn, but we knew that we had been rescued by good fortune at the last possible second. We also knew, however, that we would have to do things differently if we wanted to avoid finding ourselves in the same financial hole again. That phone call and the projects it initiated gave the company a shot in the heart, allowing it to start pumping blood again. It was a second life, and like for people who have had a near-death experience, it was a chance to change, to rebuild, to prosper. It was our opportunity to fix bad habits and rethink everything that had nearly killed us.

I didn't have a blueprint for how we would rebuild our business. All I knew was that I didn't want to go bankrupt again. To ensure that we wouldn't, I decided that our only hope for survival was to do things differently than every other company around us and differently than what we'd done before.

As an entrepreneur just starting out, I quickly learned that you have to do the jobs of every employee you can't afford to hire. If you need three employees to push your fledgling company forward, then you have to work three shifts. That's exactly what I did for the first year after securing the project that kept us afloat; I worked sixteen to eighteen hours a day, seven days a week, doing sales all day and juggling administrative work and various operational responsibilities at night, thus coining one of my most famous phrases: if you want to live well, then you'll have to sleep bad.

Things started to work out. However, it didn't take long before I saw that I could not grow the company exponentially if I didn't have time to create new streams of business, because one was not yet enough. That's when I began to imagine a new model for entrepreneurship, one which would consist of distinct business units that all fed off one another and drove revenue back to the company but, most importantly, would be led by other entrepreneurs who had their own ideas and were hungry for growth. If I had hired a person under the typical boss-employee model, I only would have been getting someone who needed me to give them orders and closely supervise the quality of their work. I knew I couldn't devote the necessary time to that type of relationship and continue growing the company at the same time. I had to invent a new kind of business model that wouldn't require that so much of my time and focus be taken away from my primary business unit, which at the time was conducting market research for real estate developers.

I caught word of an old friend I had gone to college with whose own self-started business was failing. I approached him with an idea. I would let him run a second business unit that I wanted to create, and he would keep a percentage of whatever profit that unit generated. The more profits he could produce for that unit, the more money he would pocket for himself.

That may sound like a simple system in theory, but it's actually a complicated process to implement. If we think of it in terms of biology, what I was attempting to create was akin to cellular division. I didn't want to create a larger organism predicated upon one business idea. I wanted to duplicate our company's DNA by bringing in other entrepreneurs who could build and maintain new business units.

Indeed, this was a radical idea. In stark contrast, most companies aim to grow vertically, building themselves on a hierarchical formation in which the owner, CEO, and other executives sit atop one business idea and issue commands meant to grow that idea. Those commands eventually trickle down through a series of department managers and employees who are ultimately tasked with making them work. I wanted to grow my company horizontally, meaning we would be an organization comprised of many different businesses that would all be driven by entrepreneurs, not managers—a company of semiautonomous but related businesses.

During the first year of this experiment with my old college classmate, something remarkable happened. I had predicted that his business unit would account for 5 percent of our total revenue, but in actuality, it resulted in 40 percent of our total revenue by the end of our second year together. I knew then that I was onto something. If we duplicated the model, then, in theory, our revenues would increase in tandem with the number of successful units we created. My cell division theory for business was working.

What I realized quickly was that in a hierarchical traditional structure, the boss is the bottleneck and reduces the speed of everything. Since decisions have to pass through the boss (and maybe some other desks before that), decisions become slow.

In a hierarchical traditional structure, the boss is the bottleneck and reduces the speed of everything.

In the NOMEG model, business unit leaders are completely autonomous and report only to the board, allowing them to harness the speed and agility necessary to support rapid and sustainable growth in today's market. (We will speak about talent in the next chapter.)

When I created the first business unit (outside my own), I did not think of the system. I could not handle one more thing on my plate. I was completely overworked and assumed that if that business unit was 5 percent of the company's revenue, even if it failed, there would be no harm done. That's why I gave it complete freedom. Because this model was born out of freedom, you can really feel that entrepreneurial drive from business unit leaders.

We spent roughly seven years working hard within our business units while constantly trying to create new ones. I was truly exhausted. Since 99 percent of my time was spent in operations, it was hard to create new businesses. We found that we often had to try several ideas to get one additional business unit running, but finding the time to be creative and experiment with an idea was incredibly rare. Remember that NOMEG companies are profitable, so running a lean operation is an important part of the equation.

After those years of spending most of my time toiling in operations, I reached a very difficult point in my life. At the time, my wife was pregnant with our second child. One day she called and told me that the doctor had some bad news about our pregnancy. We rushed to the doctor's office, where they proceeded to tell us that our baby had a heart condition and that she might need surgery immediately after she was born. The doctor also advised us to seek out the best medical attention because of the severity and rarity of the situation. As soon as I heard this, I spoke to my partners and decided that I would move temporarily to the US to assemble the best medical team for my daughter. In doing so, we agreed that I would step away from the company completely for at least three months.

Tragically, my daughter would only spend one week with us. She would not survive that surgery. My wife and I were devastated, and I had to be replaced inside the company while I grieved.

My partners named a new business unit leader. To my surprise, my replacement improved every key performance indicator (KPI) within the unit. Simply put, she was much better at running the unit than I was.

When I finally returned to the company, my partners insisted that there was no point in me taking back the operations of that business unit. She was the better operator, and we agreed that the unit would run with greater order and profitability if she remained in charge.

That was a blow to me at first, of course. *Where does that leave me?* I thought. *What am I to do?* After some reflection and discussions with my partners, we decided that I should be in charge of innovation. I came back to the office as the "chief future officer," with one job description: find more businesses. This meant I was to be constantly looking ahead, analyzing trends, anticipating, predicting, and creating (there was a lot of room for creativity). This would give me time to find more than one idea that could be successful.

As it turned out, that decision, though painful at first, was actually the best thing for me. Had I never left my position within the company, I don't believe I ever would have advanced the NOMEG model and found my calling as a thought leader and business creator.

In a conventional company, there is just one business. But in a neural company, there are many businesses. The strength of the NOMEG system relies on the speed of business creation. There is no one primary business that defines the company. Instead, the company is defined as a network of different business units that are all working in tandem. When I was finally freed of operations, I would have time to really accelerate the Edison Chain.

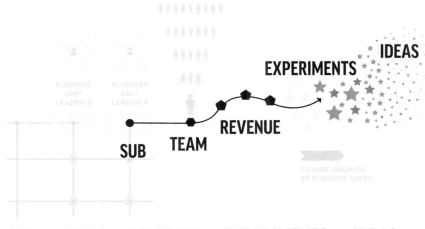

SUB > TEAM > REVENUE > EXPERIMENTS > IDEAS

As you now look more closely at the graph, you quickly realize that the Edison Chain is actually created by a system where ideas are turned into experiments, experiments are taken to revenue models, and then a leader is put in place to pursue that model. As I had complete freedom, I could finally set up a team dedicated to creating that future. In short, we operated under a simple formula: **Ideas → Experiments → Revenue Generation**.

If an idea wasn't doing well in the experimentation phase, we let it die and would begin the process anew.

You should only invest money into a business innovation once the uncertainty and risk around that idea has been reduced. That's part of the NOMEG system's "magic," as it enables you to gather enough quality data to lower uncertainty and minimize financial risk when investing in a new idea.

One mistake people often make lies in investing a lot of money into an idea without being certain whether the market wants it. In fact, that is the main cause of product failure. I never invest in a business idea that requires large sums of money up front. Instead, NOMEG focuses on the process of bringing uncertainty down before making any significant financial investment. As you bring uncertainty down, you can increase the spending levels of research and development and marketing. The innovations we look for are the ones that start with experiments, and then we increase spending levels as we diminish the uncertainty around market risks. Remember I told you about the ideas of Eric Ries? You might already have identified the concept of the MVP, or the minimum viable product.

Never invest in good ideas; invest only in good data. You can spend small amounts of money for the experiments needed to test out the idea on a specific market, but serious money should be reserved for ideas that have solid data. That data should tell you the wants and needs of the intended market, what price point(s) the market would be willing to withstand, and what it would cost to bring the idea to market (e.g., production and marketing costs, distribution costs, legal expenses, etc.). That data is necessary to have to ensure the idea's profitability as much as possible. The stronger the data, the stronger the investment.

Now that you understand this concept, you may be wondering where the process of investing in a business unit begins. The answer can be found in what I call **market hallucinations**. By that I mean any idea with the potential to disrupt a market. The word *hallucination* is important here because it evokes a sense of madness; most brilliant innovations sound crazy in the beginning. Who was the one who thought, some years ago, that a streaming television series set in the 1980s about a group of preteens from a small rural town fighting against a dark monster concealed by the US government would actually work? The Duffer brothers did. They called it *Stranger Things*, and it became a smash hit. This part connects deeply with my creative side, that crazy side that comes out when I create social media content or speak in front of thousands of people. A boring idea isn't going to be a disruptive market innovation. That's why I look for ideas that are completely different from what everyone else believes within a particular market.

The magic in the NOMEG system begins with these market hallucinations, but the profitability of NOMEG's investment strategy comes from carefully testing these hallucinations to ensure their financial success prior to putting any significant amount of money into them. We accomplish this balance between crazy thinking and sound business decisions by pushing ideas through the five distinct phases of business unit development: market hallucination, hypothesis, experimentation, data collection, and execution/modification.

As we discussed, the first phase is market hallucination, in which we search for the most disruptive and unconventional ideas we can imagine. Once we have a strong market hallucination in mind, we carry it into the second phase of development: **hypothesis**. The hypothesis phase is where you create a reasonable premise for why the hallucination would generate a profit. In this phase, all that we want to do is examine the feasibility of turning our hallucination into a viable business opportunity.

I'll give you another example, from Alberto Savoia's 2019 book *The Right It: Why So Many Ideas Fail and How to Make Sure Yours Succeed.*

In the book, Savoia presents a hypothetical story in which his market hallucination is a beer for dogs. If dog beer sounds bizarre, worrisome, brilliant, or some combination of the three to you, then the hallucination has done its job. It got your attention because it's something that you have never seen before or perhaps never even thought about.

As with all market hallucinations, the problem with such a strange idea is knowing whether it's a worthy business idea to pursue in real life. Savoia answers that uncertainty by explaining a concept that he calls the "XYZ hypothesis"—which, along with Dan Olsen's *The Lean Product Playbook*; Alexander Osterwalder, Yves Pigneur, Fred Etiemble, and Alan Smith's *The Invincible Company*; and Eric Ries's *The Lean Startup,* completely changed the way I see businesses today.

The purpose of his XYZ hypothesis is to turn a conventional hypothesis into something you can measure from a business standpoint. In other words, the XYZ hypothesis represents the hypothesis phase of developing a theory but with a more business-centric approach in mind.

Savoia's market hallucination is a beer made for dogs. His hypothesis is that "some pet owners don't like to drink alone; many would buy dog beer for their best friend to drink with them." To test this hypothesis, he moves into the third phase of experimentation by conducting a survey among a sample size of his target market: dog owners. The survey finds that 15 percent of dog owners would buy a six-pack of dog beer for $4 when they buy dog food. Those findings represent enough of a market interest and opportunity for profitability to pursue the idea on a small scale. To further test the hallucination, Savoia proposes producing a small batch of dog beer and selling six-packs of the product for $4 at a local pet store, placing the displays alongside dog food.

Once those experiments are completed, Savoia would presumably have collected enough data (the fourth phase) to decide whether he should seriously invest in executing the idea on a larger scale and/or modifying it to attain greater profitability, the fifth and final phase of developing a new business unit.

There is a vast array of experiments you can use to test your hypotheses, but it's best to conduct multiple experiments of different types with a distinct question in mind for each experiment to answer (e.g., market demand, product quality, customer satisfaction, price point, etc.). We often use an experiment that's commonly referred to as a clickable prototype. Just like it sounds, a clickable prototype allows you to test designs, features, and ideas related to websites, apps, or any other digital customer experiences. This type of experiment is extremely important for businesses that sell products and/or services on a digital platform. Ever since people began spending more time and money on online shopping, mountain-size piles of market research have been collected on the most effective ways to engage people in a digital world. From the best colors and fonts to the ideal image content, from the streamlining of the purchase process to the ways user data is collected and used, companies wishing to conduct business online have a wealth of tried-and-true methods to choose from when designing their own platforms. We like a company called Figma because it enables us to quickly and easily design webpages that are capable of simulating the complete customer experience. That's a great tool to have when you want to test different designs, layouts, or functions. It's especially helpful when experimenting with who to design your digital experience for, as you may want to build multiple versions of the same site for different audience types. Companies like Figma (and there are many others like it out there) allow us to build a page or app in a matter of hours and then invite people to use it so we can see what features they like and don't like as well as what features give us the best results for our desired goal(s).

Another experiment type we like a lot is called the **single feature MVP**. This experiment aims to uncover which of your products or services is your most important. Note that I didn't say your most profitable. Profit is important, sure, but many times your most important product or service may not be your *most profitable* one on its own but rather is the one that generates the most engagement and/or loyalty from customers. A restaurant that gives away fresh bread or chips and salsa while you wait for your meal isn't making money on those items, but they help to ensure customer satisfaction. The more satisfied guests are at the end of their dining experience, the more likely they are to eat at your restaurant again. The single feature MVP experiment is where you test for that single most important business offering, which you can then build more offerings around to increase and sustain customer spending. Think of it like a Swiss Army knife. Technically, it's a knife. Its most important feature is the knife because that's what most people who own one use the most. Other features like the screwdriver, the bottle opener, the mini saw, etc. are nice bonuses, but if the knife itself were junk, how many people do you think would buy one? You aren't buying a Swiss Army knife for those tiny scissors or the nail file. You're buying it because you need a knife, but you appreciate all the convenient tools that come along with it.

A **mash-up** is another helpful experiment that we most often use when designing software, but you can apply this technique to other ideas as well. A mash-up takes existing products and combines certain elements from them to create a new product. If you want to test something besides software, a mash-up experiment is the simple process of taking basic information from an existing product or service, examining its details to find the part(s) you like most, and then tweaking it to serve your needs. You are basically building a Frankenstein's monster with the best used parts from products, services, and ideas that have already proven to be successful in practice.

The **concierge prototype**, also known as a *Wizard of Oz* **experiment**, is a type of experiment in which you manipulate a test scenario in such a way that a product or service appears to exist to the participant but, in reality, does not yet exist. For example, you may manually perform a task but tell your sample group that the task was performed by a machine. Savoia describes an experiment in which people put unfolded clothes into a machine and were told that the machine would automatically fold them. Behind the machine and out of view from the participants, a person folded the clothes by hand and put them back into the machine for the participant to retrieve. The most common purpose of this type of experiment is to test the demand for a specific type of technology before it actually exists.

There are also many ways to test an idea that don't require an extravagant production. **Crowdfunding**, for example, is a relatively popular experiment for entrepreneurs today because it allows you to reach many people of all types quickly and cheaply, with the purpose of gaining small financial donations from lots of people in order to launch a product or service. Many business ideas have got off the ground because of crowdfunding. I personally love it because it allows you to test the demand for an idea and generate capital for it simultaneously.

For a product that already exists, **simulated presales** are a great way to test your product against competitors and gain feedback from your target buyer. We bring participants into a room with three tables, each with a different product sitting on it. At each table we have a salesperson who explains the details of the product on their table to the participant. Once the participant has visited each table, we interview them to see which product they would buy and why.

If I had to tell an organization or entrepreneur in trouble to do just one thing, it would be to experiment more. Experiment a lot more. What slows so many people down when looking for innovations for their business is their fear-based obsession with overanalysis. In those cases, it's not always true that the person is antichange but rather that they are so risk averse that they create more risk to

Experiment a lot more.

themselves by spending too much time analyzing every decision. Rather than making small, incremental changes, testing them out, and seeing what happens through actual results, they theorize about the changes until it's too late to make them.

Successful innovations are made by taking small, measured risks, assessing their outcomes, and then iterating the process until you achieve the desired results. Innovation requires a willingness to try new ideas that are likely to fail, but by experimenting with them in small doses, the learning is more like a paper cut than an amputation.

Building, Linking, and Managing a Neural Network

Strategic business units (SBUs) like the ones I'm describing are not an entirely new concept, mind you. The idea has bounced around MBA programs and in business theory circles since at least the 1970s, mostly as an executive tool for assessing the profitability of specific product lines and/or market segments held by a large corporation. SBUs are rarely, if ever, taught to be used by small entrepreneurial companies for the purposes of building a business.

In both university programs and business books, portfolio selection strategies are rarely discussed either. Knowing which business ideas we should dedicate ourselves to is critical to any kind of entrepreneurial success. When you are inside a business, opportunities to create or expand on other ideas or units arise all the time, but they are difficult to see if you are too busy managing day-to-day duties or are too fixated on one particular unit or aspect of the business. The challenge for companies using business units is discovering opportunities that can both complement an existing unit and link itself to the company's main service or product to boost its overall value. It takes a lot of vision and knowledge to juggle all those needs simultaneously, and yet portfolio selection is nearly nonexistent in commonplace business discourse.

Most business "experts" swear on the idea of a core business being the key to entrepreneurial triumph. What they mean is that you have to have a main business and then maybe a secondary business(es) around it. They look at your main business as the sun and all your other business ideas as small planets that need to orbit your "sun" without ever overshadowing it. The problem with such an antiquated approach is the speed at which businesses progress, regress, and evolve today. A secondary business can reach the same size as the core business in a very short time. It is not a question of replacing one core with another and growing to have two or three core businesses but of understanding that you are operating a business chain and that chain now has a new link. It's a shared force, altogether propelling you toward a bigger, better, more durable company.

There is a difference between this:

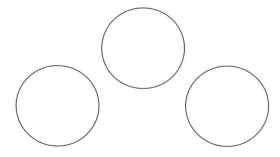

and this:

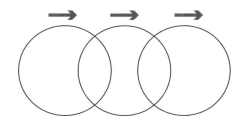

I don't mean that you should think of this business chain as a collection of any and all businesses, either. I would never ask you to amass a fortune and then start opening whatever business came to mind just because you thought it had the potential to be profitable—even if that were true. A grocery store, a computer repair shop, and a nail salon are not links in the same chain but rather three different chains entirely. They are core businesses that are so different that they cannot adequately feed off one another. They are different universes existing on their own. In a literal chain, one link serves to give strength to the next. In a business chain, one link serves to add value to the next, thus multiplying your efforts.

The units have to be related in terms of your overall industry focus (real estate in 4S's case), but they do not have to be related along service or product lines. In fact, you want a wide range of services and products to offer your respective industry. The units themselves are ultimately driven by the creativity and interest of the unit leader.

Take my first company, 4S Real Estate, as an example. Unquestionably, 4S is successful because I was able to chain small businesses together. The synergy between them produced joint growth across all these so-called links. While 4S began as a market research company for the real estate sector, over time, I discovered new business opportunities related to real estate that 4S could serve by building out separate business units. We now offer thirteen different services ranging from design to marketing to logistics and planning in eighteen offices across Latin America. If you tried to define what 4S is, you would probably say that it's a real estate consultancy firm, but inside it is a chain of thirteen different business units that all feed off one another. Those thirteen businesses encompass markets ranging from digital technology services to marketing and branding to architectural design to property management to purchasing and logistics to construction and more.

When you set out to start a business chain, the first link is critical. That first link should be capable of opening the door to many other business opportunities. When your first link is solid enough to attach additional links to, then you will see the beauty of creating business chains rather than *a* business. You will also see how the Neural Organization Model transforms a company from a stiff, authoritarian-like structure with branches, departments, and never-ending power levels operating vertically (like an office building, where the CEO occupies the top floor and the least important employee works in the basement. That structure hurts everyone and limits creativity and initiative and promotes cutthroat attitudes that damage the company's dynamic) into a network of self-driven units—an orchestra of entrepreneurs, if you will, in which a COO acts as its conductor and a CEO serves as its composer. Similar to biological functions, we are streamlining the company into a system of independent cells that form, grow, and break apart based on the success of a single idea or opportunity.

However, the CEO's role in the NOMEG model is perhaps the most important part of the model. It's just different than the traditional business models, in which the CEO stands in a hierarchical position, tasked with exploiting the business in a dictator-style role, giving orders and expressing goals that should trickle down all the way to the bottom to get results from the way the business currently operates. The CEO's role in the NOMEG model, on the other hand, is an explorative one. In this new system, the CEO must maintain an entrepreneurial mindset, with a mission to expand the company's field of business.

Getting this new role for the CEO right is critical to the model's success, and it requires a person to have a passion for exploration and expansion. I think of the old role of a CEO as the king who stays in the very back of his army watching from a hilltop as his troops fight to win the battle. The

NOMEG CEO, on the other hand, is like William Wallace as depicted in the film *Braveheart*. The NOMEG CEO inspires their troops and leads them into battle directly. The new CEO is doing the innovation and running the chaos. This is a whole new breed of CEOs because it's much harder to manage the chaos of innovation and exploration than it is to manage the order of a stable business's daily operations.

When I introduce this idea to millennial or centennial entrepreneurs, they often get very excited. They have a sense of equality and confidence. On the other hand, when I present it to career executive types, most likely Gen Xers who still dress up for work and even carry brown briefcases like their dads did, they typically grow concerned and begin to consider an important question: "How is a CEO supposed to manage a company like this?" Gen Xers are so used to looking up or down that the concept confuses them. The answer is that CEOs don't manage a company like that. The key to the sustainability of a neural-structured company is its team. Let go of the idea of the subordinate! Who you hire, trust, and allow to lead is critical. I'll show you how.

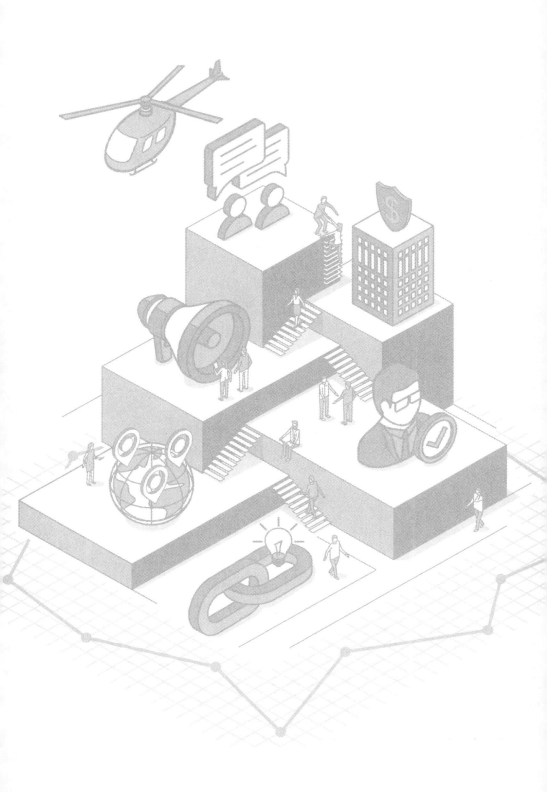

CHAPTER TWO

GETTING PEOPLE RIGHT

The Talent System

If you haven't figured it out already, one of the most vital components to the NOMEG model is talent (aka your team). Companies using NOMEG need creative, entrepreneurial-minded people in several places, from interns to strategic business unit leaders to the COO and CEO.

Fairly early on in our own transformation to the NOMEG model, we thought we could get the right people for our system by sticking to the traditional method and just hiring for every position directly from the general talent pool, LinkedIn-type posts, scouting, and feeding off universities—all with basic, old-school job proposals based on salaries and benefits. The learning curve, as it turned out, was steeper than we'd thought. Over time, we developed a talent system that produced more consistent results in terms of both company-talent alignment and the success the people we hired ultimately had within the company. Basically, we started getting the best of the best without spending like the rest. I divide that system into four components, which together build and maintain what I call the **talent machine** or **leader factory**:

1. Culture

2. Diamond Mining

3. Leadership Development

4. Leadership Empowerment

Before we discuss how to solve the talent problem, let me clarify something that's critical to the proper foundation of NOMEG's talent machine model. A strong and healthy company culture is essential to any good talent recruitment, creation, and retention program. You want people to want to work with you because you're cool enough, because your identity and your brand are appealing, and because they feel connected to your identity and brand. You want to have that Google vibe that everyone still talks about. Don't get me wrong. Money is still a major factor, and the biggest companies out there can still lure in talent with gigantic salaries. But we also learned that we could beat them with our "sexiness." Now, there are hundreds of books out there that explain nothing else but company culture. This is not one of them although I agree that your culture has a major impact on the success of a company.

To understand NOMEG's approach to culture and growth from a talent perspective, you should familiarize yourself with one core principle: each person you hire must be so good that you would feel comfortable working for them.

That may sound frightening and radical to some, but exponential growth in any organization cannot be achieved without exceptional talent. That means you should be attracting and then hiring the very best people you can find. Think of it this way: if you feel like you're the smartest, most talented person at every position within your own company, then something has gone horribly wrong. You're stuck in the hierarchical model of the past. If you like it—the power over someone, that is—I would recommend you seek professional help since we don't live in those times anymore.

Culture often plays a starring role in a company's ability to attract top talent, and it's certainly one of the biggest factors in keeping them once they're there. Don't just ask a new team member what they can bring to the table; rather, ask yourself what you can offer to them. A great culture and the company's success in the talent market as a whole is achieved through its **employee value proposition (EVP)**.

CVP < EVP

Customer Value Proposition   Employee Value Proposition

What you just read is not a printing error. I truly believe that the employee value proposition is more important than the customer value proposition. Please, I urge you to take that notion that "the customer comes first" and think about your employees as well. You're going to think it's absurd, but that's why I'm here writing this book. Let me explain.

During the growth of a company—a process that I have experienced on multiple occasions—it is easy to get a strong starting spot within a particular market if you understand the game of experimentation. As you open that spot in the market, the real challenge will come: to serve the market at the level of competitiveness it requires. Since you're a newcomer to the market, you'll need to be more creative, innovative, crazy, bold, smart, etc. than your competitors to gain a share of that market's consumer base. You will need to come up with new products, services, and creative marketing to reach out to more people or to engage with your existing market; you will also need to refine or improve your communication channels. This will only be accomplished quickly if you assemble an extraordinary team. A team will allow you to grow, and the quality of that team will often determine the size and speed of the growth. A weak or nonexistent team will result in the shrinking of any past growth and, eventually, the company's death.

The first step in building your talent generator is accepting one truth: EVP will allow you to attract extraordinary talent within a cost-structure you can afford during your initial period of growth.

The second part has to do with your culture. The EVP is the part that is seen from outside the culture, but it goes much further. The culture of your company is made up of a complete series of protocols, rituals, values, traditions, and ways of collaborating that are practiced internally. Culture is the secret to building, retaining, and unleashing great talent in your company.

The third part has to do with how culture materializes in the organization, in its implementation. Most people who live in the past (or in the lies told by business schools and others) believe that culture emanates from the top and cascades down onto everyone else, that the supreme leader from high above (usually the company's founder, who is seen as a saint and their words taken as gospel) pours it over the organization and everyone else swims in it. Nothing could be further from reality! Culture is evident in the way work teams operate within the company. The secret is in having committed collaborators. It's the talent you bring in and how that talent is assembled into teams that have the most influence on culture. Culture forms in a groundswell from the talent itself, not from a waterfall controlled by the top of an outdated hierarchy pouring over them. Therefore, the backbone of the NOMEG model looks like this:

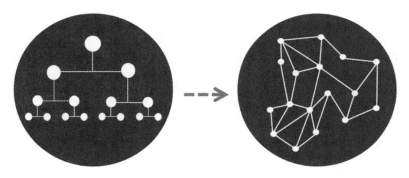

Teams → Culture → EVP

With this diagram, I want to make it very clear that it is not about selling smoke screens to people. It is not about doing a great advertising campaign that shows a fake EVP just out of a desire to attract the attention of the talent market.

EVP resulting from great culture is the strategic secret of exponentially growing companies.

I will take you by the hand in the process that helped me create my own culture within the different organizations that I have built. As I said before, everything is created when you are a small company and only have a limited work team. At that time, although it may seem insignificant or even unnoticeable, in reality, the team's genetic code of collaboration is already being written. That DNA, so to speak, will determine the company's aspirations and whether it really is any different from the rest of its industry.

How do you listen to the opinion of your people? How do you construct productive work meetings? What happens at your company that sets it apart from any other company? The answers to all these questions and many more lie in the company's genetic code. Let's look at a few examples of what I mean for a better understanding of this idea.

At my education-focused company, i11 Digital, there are no assigned work spaces. If you work with (not for) me, every week you will have to sit in a different place. We have tables for three to four people, and when I am in the office, I sometimes sit side by side with one of our interns, just like the ones who took my office back at 4S. This sends a very powerful message to the organization: there are no hierarchies here.

Let me give you another example. If you follow me on social media—especially on Instagram—you will realize that my best working hours are at night. It is a message I constantly try to get out there. I don't know why, but I've always

There are no hierarchies here.

felt more comfortable and more focused around midnight. That makes morning hours too frustrating for me. That is why I tell people that the concept of waking up early, before everyone else, being a clear path to success is a myth. You have to be strategic about your time, absolutely, but waking up before the crack of dawn is a choice, not a key factor to any kind of success. Hey, if you want to start working at four in the morning, be my guest, just don't think that doing so puts you ahead of everyone else. Discovering the hours when you are most productive and prioritizing those hours in your work schedule will pave a way to more productive work (and, in turn, more professional success) over the long term. For the same reason and to be consistent with my way of working, I decided to eliminate office hours. Imagine that—working in a company where the schedule is literally defined by your preferred work hours.

When I discussed this idea with a couple of friends, they called me crazy. They told me it wouldn't work and that in three months' time, we would mount ourselves to a traditional work structure and schedule. They were almost certain that I'd have a punch card next to the main entrance. Well, we have been working without office hours or assigned seating at i11 Digital for more than a year, and it has worked exceptionally well for us.

Some Monday mornings I arrive and find the office empty. Chairs, desks, rest areas. All empty. Seeing this sight for the first time, most would believe that everything was about to collapse. However, I can also arrive on a Thursday at midnight and see the place full and everyone busy. Moments like these are when you can really see, feel, and understand the magic of this model. All these rituals, policies, processes, and ways of working and collaborating make the difference when creating a magical culture of your own. It is all very organic.

Before thinking about what and how you want to communicate your genetics to the talent market, the first thing I ask of you is to carefully analyze the working method of your teams. What makes your company different from the rest of the world? Aside from the salary, what makes it sexy?

Have you wondered what makes your way of working different? How do employees get along? Who makes the decisions in a meeting? What are your company's unwritten work rules? Is everyone allowed to speak? Is there a dress code? Is cleanliness maintained in the office? Do you allow beers and entertainment at any time of the day? How are vacation days requested? How are people measured?

There are thousands more questions like these that you can ask yourself. They are practically innumerable. What I want you to understand is that it is what you do *differently* within your organization that will ultimately differentiate it from the others. Unfortunately, when companies grow, they tend to forget the details that make them a unique entity. When you preserve that uniqueness and pass it on to your team, no matter how big it is or how much the company has grown, the famous work culture appears. There is a very powerful phrase I like that states, "Culture eats strategy for lunch," meaning that when culture exists, it can be even more important than strategy. This is true, in my opinion. While you have to put a conscious effort into building a strategy, a work culture will be created whether you put any thought or effort into it or not—and you probably won't like what you end up with if you don't.

In fact, we could even stop calling it *culture* and use another word for it, like *vibe, energy, mood,* or even *feel.* These words are closer to the meaning behind describing a place, brand, or company. How would you describe a new Californian clothing brand? How about a small coffee brewing company in Boulder, Colorado? Or a shoe brand like Atoms in NYC? When you see them from the outside (almost certainly through social media), you get a specific sense of place, purpose, and personality from them. That feeling, vibe, mood, etc. plays an increasingly influential role in attracting strong talent today.

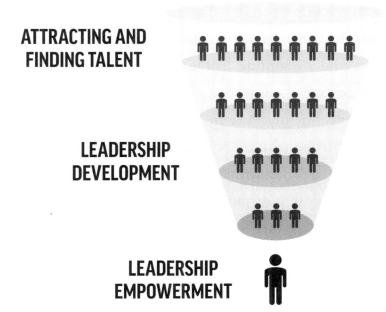

ATTRACTING AND FINDING TALENT

LEADERSHIP DEVELOPMENT

LEADERSHIP EMPOWERMENT

You may think of the link between talent and a company's overall vibe as obvious, but throughout my years of traveling around the continent to speak with entrepreneurs, talent remains the most neglected topic. Most leaders are isolated in their businesses, watching over the microorganizations that have hired many employees but not leaders. The challenge of understanding this truth is to start building an organization that is characterized by attracting and retaining leadership and talent from the job market.

For growing companies that cannot compete against larger companies in terms of compensation, I always tell them to look for young talent in the market and develop it.

When you're operating on a tighter budget, you have to rely on talent in a "green" state, in the process of maturing. You can find a diamond in the rough, so to speak, simply because no one else is looking for a diamond (i.e., a person with strong but undeveloped talent and drive) or taking an interest in polishing one up even if it does tumble into their hands. This is another secret to having an aggressively democratic EVP: it attracts impressive young talent.

The secret to NOMEG's talent machine is changing the way teams work. By creating a company-wide vibe that's unique and attractive to the types of workers you want, you are actually creating an inexhaustible source for extraordinary talent. Unlike the **Russian doll method**, in which leaders hire less talented people to insulate themselves from perceived threats to their own jobs or egos.

Building a NOMEG Leader

Maybe you've heard all those quotes that say something like, "Success as a leader is realizing your full potential." I think the mindset behind those quotes is wrong. For me, success as a leader is measured by your ability to increase the potential of those working with you, not your own.

Leaders are built, not born. That belief is now central to NOMEG's approach to leadership development. No one is a good leader simply because of their DNA. They are not "a natural born leader." That's a ridiculous idea, but unfortunately, a lot of people believe it. That's one reason why so many people think they can lead when they can't. Confidence, knowledge, boldness, interpersonal skills, decisiveness, critical thinking and innovation skills, empathy, humility—all these traits (and more) that we value in a leader can be developed. They may be easier to develop in some than in others, but I believe you can build the right leader for virtually any job. I also believe that you will build better leaders by using candidates from within your organization and by beginning their development process as soon as possible.

From a managerial perspective, developing talent from within the company for leadership roles is important for two main reasons: **compatibility** and **retention**.

Building up existing talent decreases the amount of time and resources you have to spend onboarding an external candidate, and more importantly, it lessens your chances of ending up with a leader who doesn't actually align with the company vibe or the talent they're meant to lead. If they were attracted to the company's vibe enough to seek a position with the company and succeeded in their goals and responsibilities within the company, then they're more likely to make a successful transition into a leadership role. Developing leaders from within also shows your talent that the organization will support, and make room for, their ambitions, emphasizing that there are opportunities for their continual professional, financial, and personal growth. You are showing your loyalty to them and the culture by prioritizing their development instead of bringing in someone new to skip ahead of the line.

There are five main stages comprising the NOMEG program for leadership development: **identification, motivation, empowerment, mentorship**, and **reproduction**.

IDENTIFICATION

We first have to identify who the potential leaders are. To illustrate our strategy for this mission, let me tell you a story from John Maxwell's book *The Leader's Greatest Return*. John recalls a meeting he had with a man named Bob, who owns a business making custom guitars. Bob tells John that he wants to find someone who is better at making guitars than he is but that he also wants them to be self-taught. He wants them to be a professional guitar player, and he wants them to have played on stage with some of the "big ones" (i.e., world-renowned guitar players). Bob says that he also wants this employee to be a "great human being," know the complete history of guitars, and have twenty years of professional experience as a guitar builder. Oh, and Bob wants them to currently live in San Diego. To recap, Bob wants a famous, professional guitar player who fits his definition of a "great human being," expects to find them in a geographically specific talent pool, and wants them to have at least twenty years of professional experience building guitars. How do you think Bob's search for an employee is going to go?

Most of us are not as out of touch with reality as Bob appears to be, but many of us do begin our search for the right person with a list of ideal qualities we're looking for in a candidate. And it's not a rare occurrence to watch that list magically grow the more we analyze our fantasy hire. Delegating is a common problem among leaders, and I hear over and over again from them that they *would* delegate more but they just can't find the right person. That's a bullshit excuse. They haven't found the right (read: perfect) person, because they don't exist. The right person may exist in your head, but they don't exist in real life. That's why you have to reframe your mindset and figure out how you can build that person yourself.

That's a hard mindset to commit to because it's a slower process that requires more of your time and energy. For the big corporations operating under the traditional talent model, truly developing talent to their maximum potential is seen as a waste of time and money. They believe they can hire someone with a strong corporate pedigree, essentially a plug-and-play scenario. They look for someone whose résumé and interviews confirm to them that they went to the right schools, received the right degrees, got the right internships, and spent the right amount of time in the right positions at the right companies in the right industries. If all looks right, they hire them. That strategy often works out okay for them because there is so little difference in the general culture between one corporate behemoth and another. The setting may change, but the systems, mindsets, and operating procedures remain largely the same. Their goal is to find someone that can dissolve into the ranks as quickly and quietly as possible and operate as another cog in their machine. They want it that way because they're in a hurry. They want to build a thing, whether it's a product or the company itself, today and sell it tomorrow. It's like they're still operating as mass production factories, when in reality, no one wants that anymore. No one wants to consume or to work in an old-school, generic production scheme.

I am in no hurry. I want to build companies that grow and improve naturally for life. I don't just want to build successful businesses; I want to build a kind of organism that will outlive me. I am in no hurry to build leaders, either. I want to take my time because I know that the team we build together is the most valuable part of the company. And, as an entrepreneur and mentor, it's also the most fulfilling part of the job for me.

So what do I look for in these diamonds in the rough, then? I look for these five things:

1. They must love results.

2. They are hungry for more.

3. They can tolerate and are accustomed to a lot of uncertainty.

4. They are impatient.

5. They are contagious.

I don't care about age. They can be eighteen or forty-eight. I don't care about anything else outside of those five qualities. I usually notice number five (are they contagious?) first. This is the person who is always around other people and has a lot of energy, with a passionate, optimistic outlook on life. If I find that they possess the other four qualities as well, then I move to separate them from the rest of the pack.

MOTIVATION AND EMPOWERMENT

Once you have found your leader candidate, the first thing you need to do is expose them to what it feels like to be at the leadership table. Think of King Arthur and his knights gathered around their famous round table. Everyone at the table was equal. The same idea is behind NOMEG's leadership table. I put one—and only one—of these diamonds in the rough at the table at a time for three reasons.

First, I want them to experience the culture; I want them to benefit from the power of proximity. Even though they don't own any business units yet, they are meeting with other leaders, maybe for the first time, and seeing, hearing, speaking, feeling, and practicing leadership at that table. Bringing them to that table is about building up their sense of worth.

Second, I want them to know that there is a space for them. That's why it's important that they see for themselves that every major decision we make is a democratic one. Every important decision is put before this council and made with the consent of the leaders. Because I value every opinion from my leaders, I am always the last one to speak. The leadership table serves a dual purpose in that way, as it helps us make decisions and build leaders. They need to know that the company they're a part of is democratic and open to the opinions and ideas of everyone involved. Exposing them to the leadership table helps to affirm that notion.

Third, I want to know more about them. If they feel that they are listened to and respected by these leaders, then they are more likely to share their opinions and pursue their ideas with zeal. The meetings are meant to inspire, energize, inform, support, and challenge everyone, and I want to see how new leaders respond to them. I want them to feel comfortable revealing more about themselves, and giving them a space like this allows me to gain more insight into what kind of leader they may be.

Because I value every opinion from my leaders, I am always the last one to speak.

Once you believe the candidate is ready for the next level of the empowerment phase, you put them into the Edison Chain. Remember that the Edison Chain is where your ideas come from, where you test out new businesses and see whether they will be profitable. The CEO and, in a smaller capacity, the board are working with the Edison teams to make sure their experiments are creating revenue, but the success of an SBU is ultimately the responsibility of the unit's leader.

The leader candidate is not made the leader of a unit right away. They may be placed into an existing unit first to gain more experience and allow them to see how the unit is being run. After a business unit (aka experiment) produces a profit for a minimum of two quarters, then that unit is ready for a leader. Once a unit is ready for a leader (e.g., a new unit becomes profitable or another leader needs to be replaced) and if that diamond in the rough is ready, then you make them a leader. The empowerment phase is about liberation, freeing the person to make larger decisions and execute their ideas as they see fit.

MENTORSHIP

Once you empower them by appointing them to an actual leadership position, the process is not over by any means. The "diamond" will still need to sharpen their leadership skills, and they will undoubtedly need some assistance. This point marks the mentorship phase of the development process.

The French writer and aviator Antoine de Saint-Exupéry once wrote, "If you want to build a ship, don't drum up the men to gather wood, divide the work, and give orders. Instead, teach them to yearn for the vast and endless sea." Another quote from which I found inspiration for the NOMEG system comes from the US general George Patton, who said, "Never tell people how to do things. Tell them what to do, and they will surprise you with their ingenuity." These ideas are an integral part of NOMEG's mentoring strategy for developing new leaders. The CEO and COO serve as mentors to the leaders. As such, you will be tasked with answering questions, providing instruction on how to do certain operational things, and offering guidance on what to do as a leader. You cannot do it for them, however, nor should you tell them how to do everything. Both you and the new leader need to know that they're capable of taking charge, making decisions, problem solving, and producing results. If you tell them how to do everything, they won't learn nearly as much *and* they will lose confidence in themselves.

We do have a mentorship formula in place to help guide us through the process of handing over units to a new leader. We call it *IDEA*, which stands for *instruction*, *demonstration*, *exposure*, and *accountability*.

We start with instruction, meaning the mentor tells the leader how to do certain things relevant to that unit. We do *not* instruct by saying, "This is how to do XYZ." The mentor simply tells them how they do it. That kind of instruction sounds something like this: "Just so you know, this is how this business unit is run right now. You don't have to use the same system. I just want you to know that this is already working."

Then you demonstrate by doing it with them at the same time. Once you have provided instructions and demonstrated everything they need to know, then you tell the staff working in that business unit, "Everyone, this is the owner of this unit." That's the exposure they need to let their new team know that they are in charge.

The final step of turning over the unit's reins to them is establishing their accountability. We do this by introducing them to our board members and having them sign an agreement that details the expectations and consequences of their new role.

As the unit leader, it's their job to hit the unit's revenue goals. The accountability portion of their mentorship begins as soon as they take ownership of their unit. They will have a meeting with the board, during which the new leader signs an accountability agreement that details specific one-year goals for that business unit and formally states that they are the owner of that unit. Afterward, they are fully liberated. It is their business. They can do whatever they want with it, but they must reach their one-year goal(s) to keep it.

They're not completely thrown into the wild, though. We will discuss any problems they may encounter in our leadership meetings, and each quarter they will meet one-on-one with the board to review their progress and discuss any ongoing issues they're having trouble overcoming on their own. Their mentor and the board will continue helping them by providing advice, tools, and additional resources if we deem them necessary.

The main purpose of these meetings is changing their mindset. Remember, you do not want to tell them how to do things. You can tell them what to try, but the goal is changing their mindset into that of a good leader, not telling them how to lead their unit. You want to create the emotional intelligence required for leadership. You should offer advice and tips on things like managing conflict, developing teams, balancing workload, communicating, etc. But you've already given them the most powerful weapon in the mentorship arsenal: you've empowered the leader with their own unit, their own business. The most important part at that point is working with their personal beliefs around what they can or can't do. That doesn't mean there aren't consequences, though.

We approach the consequences of failure like baseball. They get three strikes. If the leader fails to reach their revenue goal for the first quarter, that's one strike. We use the meeting to understand the challenges they're having and offer our collective wisdom to them. If they still haven't met their goals after the second quarter, strike two and more mentoring. And if they fail to meet their goals after the third quarter, then the leader simply does not go to the board meeting. Instead, we use that meeting to select their replacement.

Remember that these are people who love results, so having to fire a leader is rare, but it has happened. Just because we believe that we can build people into good leaders doesn't mean that everyone responds to our efforts the same, even if the "diamond" and the mentor really believed they would. It's important to be clear on what your expectations are and what the consequences of not meeting them are. You have to remain committed to helping them meet those expectations throughout the one-year mentoring stage as well, but you must also be strict and follow through with the consequences you made clear in the beginning.

That still does not fulfill the duties of a mentor, though. You have to understand and guide your mentee as both an individual and a leader, which can prove a confusing and difficult task for anyone but especially so if you're new to the role.

The mentor's job is to find the self-criticism or self-doubt in their leader and then help them identify its source and manage it. Great leadership is the ability to act as an equalizer, which entails knowing how to behave in a given moment and what actions to take. For example, Will you empower, or will you micromanage? Should you mentor an individual, or should you fire them? A disciplined or free-form style of leadership? Lead or follow? There are times when a leader should empower, and there are times when they should micromanage. There is a time to mentor someone, and there is a time to cut them loose. There is a time to demand more discipline and a time to loosen your grip. None of these decisions should be thought of as one-or-the-other options for a given situation; rather, they represent the opposite ends of a spectrum that every good leader should be adept at maneuvering through. A great leader knows when to slide their behavior toward one of these extremes and how far.

We practice this concept in our mentorship sessions with the mentees. We analyze how they equalize the situation they're in. We want them to understand that a great leader can move all across the board, that they're not fixed points on a graph. We also may have to step in to correct that equalizer when necessary.

It's important to keep in mind that, as a mentor, you aren't there just to rattle off business knowledge, general instructions, and management tips. That's a coach's job. A coach is skill centric, serving as an educator more than anything else. When you're mentoring someone, you are life centered. Your job is to learn about the mentee's life so you can better motivate, inspire, encourage, and impart wisdom to them as well as fully develop the talents and abilities you see inside them, unpolished as they may be. You have to meet them where they are and draw out those leadership qualities you spotted in them in the first place. Your job is now to build them, often from the ground up, into the kind of leader you believe they can be.

I spend a lot of time with my leaders, especially those new to the role. I take them to lunch, meet them for coffee, bring them on trips with me, etc. I do that because it makes the time together more informal and personal than the feeling of "strictly business." I want them to talk to me about more than just business so I can have a better understanding of how to help them. To do that, I talk to them about life, who they are, who they want to become, about their personal fears, doubts, weaknesses, strengths, ambitions, etc. That is the only way to truly build a leader, no matter the organization, industry, or set of responsibilities.

REPRODUCTION

The last part of the leader development process is reproducing the leaders. When you understand how you created one leader, the next question you'll probably ask is, "How can I make that leader create another leader?" The answer is that you have to cultivate sponsorships. Sponsors are the people who have moved to the top of the organization, namely the CEO, COO, and the head of expansion, also known as the chief marketing officer (CMO). A sponsor is just a leader of leaders. Every sponsor has at least one person they are actively helping develop into a leader and, eventually, maybe even into a sponsor.

Reproducing leaders is one of the hardest parts of this process, and much of its difficulty stems from leaders being selfish with their knowledge and experience. Many people don't want to pass down the wisdom they earn, because they're afraid that they'll make it easier to replace them. Knowing that the NOMEG model is designed for continuous growth and expansion helps alleviate some of those instincts in people. A leader knows that they can progress to a sponsor, a sponsor to a CEO, COO, or other top position somewhere in the organization and so on. NOMEG isn't just about building and managing a company; it's about building a self-replicating organism that doesn't require much management at all. We want a well-oiled talent machine capable of running itself—not just to help us grow but also to help us move with greater speed and force across broader sections of industries and markets. Having a solid but flexible structure for talent affords organizations both greater agility and internal stability when expanding, morphing, and/or simply sustaining themselves.

Let's compare this idea to Silicon Valley's general model. The typical Silicon Valley company has an urgent need to drive growth, no matter what it takes. In the ideal Silicon Valley scenario, this is what happens: An entrepreneur(s) pitches an idea to investors. Enough investors like the idea, so they bankroll the company to pursue it. The entrepreneur assumes the role of founder and CEO and hires a bunch of people. Those people drive most of the growth. And then, when the company is growing, the investors sell the company and those leaders who were driving the growth move out. How are you going to keep growing if you've taken out all the magic? The magic lies in the actual heads inside of the company. If you have taken those out of the equation, then the company is worthless.

There is a lack of ownership to this method. Imagine you're the entrepreneur in this scenario. You have taken all this money from all these different investors, so you don't really own the company even though it may have been created as a result of your idea and built up by you. You hired the best people, you advance the company to a sufficient degree, and then you make a ton of money when the investors sell it. You use that money to branch off and start another company just like it, except that you take your five or six top people with you (who are most likely the real drivers behind the company's success). Now, whoever bought your old company is left with a corpse that they have to attempt to revive while simultaneously hemorrhaging money needed to support the company's existing operations.

I'm not judging this kind of model. They're doing their thing and making a lot of money doing it. But there is no long game to that model—and the long game is what drives me. Knowing that I'm creating business leaders and reimagining what a company looks like, what its functions are, how it operates, and the way individuals work is exciting. The long-term vision of NOMEG is to bring more purpose into the world. When you watch your own talent develop into leaders, reproduce an offspring of more leaders, and continue on, there's a deeper sense of success around what you're doing. Their successes will reveal the actual magic of this system. You will have built a machine that produces more than just money. It produces bold ideas, genuine leaders, and the blueprint for a culture capable of changing the world.

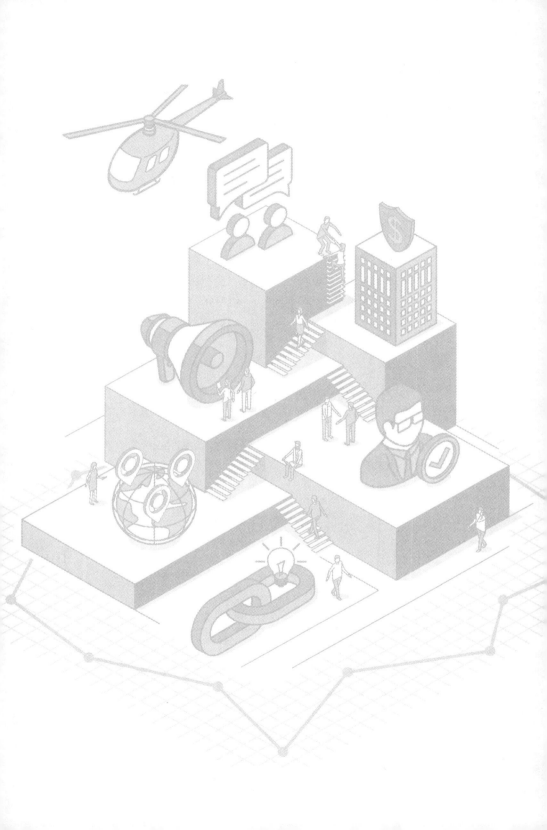

THE LEADER GENERATOR

NOMEG's Approach to Creating and Managing Talent

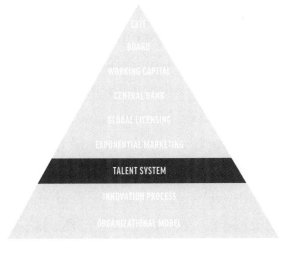

Every company, regardless of what organizational model they use, often struggles with hiring and managing talent. People are simply too unpredictable to formulate a foolproof method for either category. We found that out when we hired for a business unit leader position rather than building one from within our intern program. On paper, our top candidate to lead one of our business units had one of the best résumés I had ever seen. He had a lot of business experience, had attended great schools and done well, and he had strong references. We brought him in and conducted upward of ten interviews with him, during which he won over everyone easily. Every answer he gave us seemed like he had already known what we would ask him, and he nailed every question perfectly. We gave him technical proficiency exams, personality tests, everything. He aced every one of them. He seemed like the kind of employee that was going to change your life.

We still didn't quite trust ourselves, though, so we hired an HR consultant who would bring in candidates of her own. This guy ended up convincing the consultant that he was better than even her own candidates. This was particularly interesting because she would have received more money if we had chosen one of her candidates.

By the end, we were certain we had the right guy, so much so that we agreed to pay him the largest salary we had ever paid anyone. We bought him a company car and gave him a handsome hiring bonus too. Every perk we had, he got it.

Fast-forward to three weeks later, and we realized that as a worker, he was bad and, as a leader, he was even worse. He was very slow to implement our processes and strategies and really struggled with how to prioritize his projects. He didn't have a sense of urgency and even began fighting with people both within his unit and outside of it. In just three weeks, he had begun to destroy the entire system we were building.

We were all baffled by how this could've happened. Not only had he fooled the people inside his unit, but he had fooled the partners, the HR consultant, and me as well. We had to terminate him within a month of joining us.

That experience taught us a few things. One being that even the perfect résumé and the best interviewer in the world are by no means a good fit in our model. And the other was that we needed to create our own talent from within. Today I believe that every company should create roughly 80 percent of its talent inside the company. Let me explain why.

When I talk about the subject of talent attraction, I always think of the David versus Goliath story. All businesses that start from scratch, such as start-ups, usually enter an industry where there is already an experienced player, the proverbial "big one." So no matter what the initial investment is, the new venture will always be David fighting against well-established and powerful monsters, depending on the location and situation. Those consolidated companies can pay better wages and offer better benefits than growing companies. Hence, they are the ones that attract these stars without doing much, if anything, to reel them in. How to attract talent when you are just starting out is a critical challenge to overcome.

As you dive deep into business, you realize that ideas are actually everywhere. The hard part is not the idea but the talent that will help you bring that idea to life. Ideas need people. And people are hard to recruit, motivate, and integrate.

Imagine that you are building a basketball team. Obviously, you're looking for the most talented players, but you should also be looking for players who will complement the rest of the team.

The hard part is not the idea but the talent that will help you bring that idea to life.

What's the best way to ensure you get the right player? Should you invite them to your office and ask them, "Are you a good basketball player? Will you make a good addition to this team?" Most likely the player will answer yes to both questions, but does that mean that it's actually true? Of course not. You would give them a tryout to see how well they actually play and whether they really play well with the rest of the team. That's why we decided to focus on a trainee program rather than the traditional interview rounds to hire talent.

The neural organization model is about returning to people both their sense of personal freedom and their brains in the workplace. With the right people in the right positions performing the right jobs, a business is capable of self-duplicating multiple times over by creating semialigned business units. The problem is that most conventional business structures have been designed under the presumption that the people working within them cannot be trusted. That's true when operating in a hierarchical system that only rewards obedience. It's true for a system in which those in charge deliberately hire people who know less than they do and are less motivated than they are, for fear of introducing a threat to their own job. But a system like I'm proposing encourages fair competition and the chance for anyone to win, in stark contrast with an encrusted system determined to protect the old guards of good fortune. There are no limits to what a person can do or how far they can rise within this type of structure. It is a true meritocracy. They can even have my job if they can prove with facts and figures that they deserve it.

When I entered our building that fateful Monday, only to discover that I had been bumped out of my own office, I didn't get angry, because I realized that something far greater had happened than my losing a desk. The company vibe I had set out to create with my Neural Organization Model—one in which it's safe to take chances, it's safe to fail, and it's safe to take the initiative and make major decisions—was working. It signaled that my vision had taken hold, that it had resonated with people. My crazy experiment had progressed past any point I had ever imagined it would.

We'll discuss the mechanics in greater detail a little later, but in short, the leader of a unit is generally the product of our internship program. Interns are not made to get coffee and run errands in my companies. We accept anyone who is interested in learning about business and entrepreneurship and, for a few hours each day, we give them real work to do. The work we give them is meant to educate them and grow their work experience as well as aid in the day-to-day operations of various business units. Like most internship programs, it's a mutually beneficial relationship. Obviously, legalities around internships vary from country to country, state to state, and they frequently change, so you should check your local labor laws regularly to make sure your internship program is compliant. What I'm talking about here is a high-level view of creating an internship program that helps both the company and the interns have the best chance for success together.

Interns are divided up into rounds that last a few months, and at the end of each round, one to two are typically selected for a paid position. Their main job is to create a new business unit. Once they present an idea to me and my partners, we decide whether to fund the pursuit of that idea. If we green-light the idea, then they will enter the leadership development program we discussed earlier. If their unit reaches at least a 10 percent profitability margin, then the leader may hire others of their choosing to assist in the daily operations of the unit. As the unit's revenue grows, so does the team around it and their incomes.

Creating a culture and organizational structure that allows this kind of radical decision-making in which no one, not even the owner or CEO, is more important than anyone else takes time and a lot of mental fortitude, but it also produces some astounding results. High employee buy-in, low management needs and costs, incentivized and variable pay structures, and accelerated productivity rates are all benefits of this kind of autonomous, results-driven machine. Every person in my companies is encouraged to be creative and to take risks. Failure is not shunned; rather, it is expected and celebrated as an opportunity to learn and improve.

As an example of what I mean, 4S Real Estate was not a large company at the time that its major changes began to take root. In less than a decade, I had grown from a company of just one full-time employee (i.e., myself) to a team of roughly fifty. When I started creating this open-model system, I didn't really know that I was inventing a new way to start and operate a company. It was in the first steps of creating Frankenstein's monster that the Neural Organization was born. I needed to figure out a way that it could grow and sustain itself. I was trying to solve the very wicked problem created by outdated business schooling, capital disparities, and the suffocating, bullish competition from deep-pocketed corporations. But I had no idea that the solution would become a tool for creating more independent entrepreneurs. I was just focused on solving the problem areas found in conventional business models, one piece at a time.

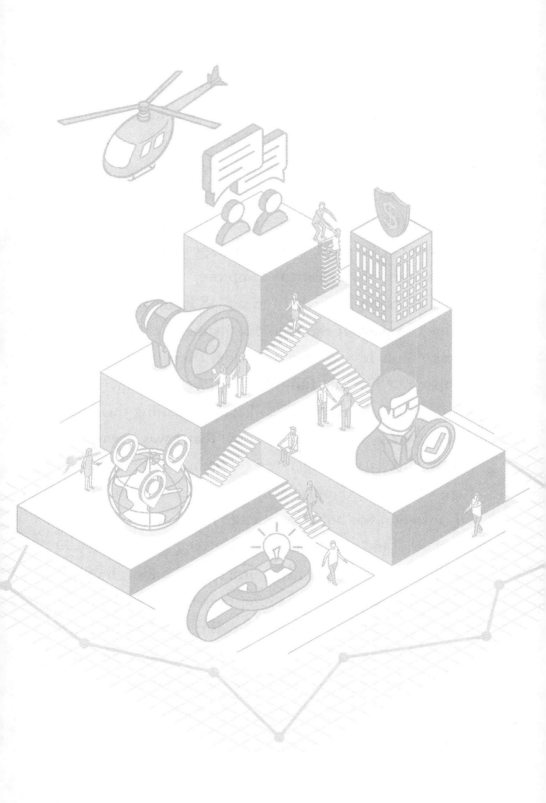

CHAPTER FOUR

DIGITAL EMPIRES

Conquest and Growth in the Modern World

No matter the industry or market in question, in business, change is one of the few certainties you can count on. You can also count on dooming your business to failure if you don't adapt to changes or innovate new shit. The S&P 500 Index measures the stock performance of the 500 largest publicly traded companies in the US. By analyzing the S&P's list of top companies since 1964, we get an excellent insight into the lifespan of dominance for large corporations.

What we find is a downward trend in corporate longevity. Companies on the S&P 500 Index in 1964 enjoyed a tenure on the list lasting thirty-three years on average, a figure that fell to twenty-four years by 2016 and is projected to shrink to between fifteen and twenty years by 2028.[1] You read that correctly: in less than ten years from now, the lifespan of the average top 500 company in the US could be nearly a decade shorter than it is today. That's how fast change is happening now; even extremely successful businesses are breaking apart, selling themselves to megacorporations or just going under because they can't keep up with the speed of change in their respective markets. Companies are morphing, mutating, and/or failing much quicker today than they were just five years ago, meaning that adaptability and innovation are more critical now than ever.

At the same time, exponential growth is occurring much, much faster. Companies are reaching large-scale results at lightning speeds, especially when compared with their progress reports from ten, twenty, and fifty years ago. Look at technology companies as an example. It took the telephone seventy-five years to reach fifty million users, yet it took Facebook just three years to reach the same number. Likewise, it took Facebook nearly eight years to gain one billion users and just three years for TikTok to reach the

---

1   INNOSIGHT, "2021 Corporate Longevity Forecast," accessed October 20, 2021, https://www.innosight.com/insight/creative-destruction/.

same milestone. We are connected on a global level today, and capabilities such as instant mass communication and increasingly affordable and accessible technologies are opening up billions of potential customers in a wide range of markets and industries. That is one reason behind such explosions in exponential growth.

I became interested in the idea of exponential growth and how to achieve it several years ago when I was trying to bring my companies' presence to the global stage. I read many books on the topic, but the five that were the most influential to me are *Exponential Organizations* by Salim Ismail; *The Future Is Faster Than You Think* by Peter Diamandis and Steven Kotler; *Beyond Disruption* by Jean-Marie Dru; *No Ordinary Disruption* by James Manyika, Jonathan Woetzel, and Richard Dobbs; and *Zero to One* by Peter Thiel. These books helped me envision and execute many of the concepts for exponential growth that we use in my companies today.

But before we go any further, let's define what **exponential growth** actually means for our purposes here. Exponential growth is a reference to the rate of change for a given quantity (e.g., revenue, number of employees, costs, users/customers, assets, etc.). Specifically, it means that a quantity's rate of change is proportional to the quantity itself, meaning that it doubles, triples, etc. in quantity over the same length of time being measured. So if your company's revenues doubled from the first to the second quarter and quadrupled between the third and fourth quarters, then your company would be experiencing consistent exponential growth for the year.

Because exponential growth is occurring much faster compared with past decades, there is also greater potential for new and/or smaller companies to rise to the ranks of the largest corporations in the world in much less time. It was common for a company to need twenty years or more to land itself on a list like the S&P 500, but now we're seeing companies reach the same kind of growth in two or three years.

While 4S Group gave me the opportunity to understand, create, and implement the neural organization model, my digital education company, i11 Digital, has given me the opportunity to really understand exponential growth by seeing it play out so dramatically firsthand. With i11, I had already built NOMEG and knew how to implement it in a company, saving me countless hours of time and countless resources spent on research and trial-and-error tactics to get the model up and running properly. i11 was born as a NOMEG company, and as such, it hit the ground running toward exponential growth from its inception. In two years, i11 was making as much revenue as 4S Group was making after its first ten years in business.

A tale about rice and a king may help further explain the concept of exponential growth. Legend has it that there was once a ruler in India who loved to make bets on his chess matches. One day, a challenger came forward and bet the ruler that he could beat him in a game of chess. The ruler asked him, "What's the prize?" The challenger told him that he wanted one grain of rice for the first square he took, but the quantity of rice must double for each square he won thereafter. The ruler laughed at this low wager and agreed to play him. The challenger won the match and returned several days later to collect his payment. When the ruler asked his treasurer why the man had not been paid, his treasurer told him that it was impossible to pay him, adding, "You would have to cover all of India in a meter of rice to pay him what he's owed."

We tend to think of exponential growth in terms of $1 + 1 + 1 + 1$ and so on. In reality, it is $1 + 1 = 2$, $2 + 2 = 4$, $4 + 4 = 8$, $8 + 8 = 16$, $16 + 16 = 32$ and so on. So the challenger in the ruler's chess match was not gaining one or two additional pieces of rice for each square he won; he was carrying over the previous square's quantity of rice and then doubling it every time he won a new square. Of course, I don't believe he could have won enough rice to actually cover all of India a meter thick, but the tale is meant as a metaphor to illustrate how quickly exponential growth can occur.

Exponential growth isn't just about money, either. We're living in an age now that is seeing exponential growth in information, as well. The amount of information we have access to is increasing at a rate that is hard to comprehend. A zettabyte, for instance, is a measurement of digital storage capacity that equates to 1 sextillion bytes (aka 10^{21} or 1,000,000,000,000,000,000,000 bytes—equal to 1 trillion gigabytes). In 2005, the amount of digital information created worldwide was 0.1 zettabytes. By 2020, that number rose to 47 zettabytes, and by 2027 it is expected to reach 163 zettabytes. That is exponential growth at warp speed, and it's all being powered by the ideas of individuals.

That amount of information is astounding. It's physically impossible to see, hear, or read all that information in a lifetime, so we must choose what's important or credible to us and then try to absorb as much of it as we can. When you change to an ecosystem that is based in information, the speed of growth becomes exponential.

The Six Ds of Exponential Organizations

We are information-enabling everything. That creates a rich opportunity for deception and confusion, but it also creates an expansive landscape of knowledge and inspiration. The educational and innovation consultancy organization Singularity Universe breaks down the digital information world into six divisions it calls "The 6 Ds of Exponential Organizations," which consist of the following categories: digitized, deceptive, disruptive, demonetized, dematerialized, and democratized.

A brief explanation of Singularity's model is that when something becomes **digitized**, it is classified as *information*. Unfortunately, when something becomes information, it often becomes **deceptive** because the technology is not yet usable for the masses. When a camera used to cost thousands of dollars and could only take a handful of pictures before another roll of film was required, it was a contraption used only by the very wealthy or the professional photographer. But the camera grew in popularity alongside technological advancements that made it easier to use and cheaper to purchase.

As technology progresses, a product or service enters the **disruptive** stage. A smart phone, for instance, was able to develop itself into a tool for making phone calls, sending and receiving text messages and emails, playing music, and taking quality photographs, among other functions. Once people could take quality photos with their phone, they had little need to buy and carry with them a contraption that could only take similar-quality photos.

As the technology advances, money is increasingly removed from the equation to the point of **demonetization.** Software is relatively free to distribute, and when it is made widely available, it's often made free to gain more users. Monetization comes through software add-ons, hardware, advertisements, and donations.

Once demonetization is achieved, we enter into **dematerialization and democratization.** As you might have assumed, this stage refers to the point at which digitization has ultimately led to all people having free and easy access to information.

When you look at all this, you can begin to see that our world is changing from a commercial environment of atoms to one of bytes. An alarm clock, a compass, a thermometer, a stereo—all these things and much more are now available as an app for your phone. We have essentially created a digital twin for physical items that can be found in most homes throughout the world. The difference between the physical objects (i.e., the atom-based shit) and the app is that once you build the app, you can reproduce it as many times as you want for almost $0 in production costs. For example, you can "manufacture," promote, and distribute millions of digital alarm clocks essentially for free when compared with manufacturing, promoting, and distributing physical alarm clocks.

The quality of technology that exists in our global society today ultimately means that we are approaching a "zero marginal cost society." This is important because once you have a zero marginal cost society, all the rules begin to change because the rules of "The Man," or traditional economics, no longer apply. Take a 2014 tweet from Airbnb's CEO, Brian Chesky, as an example: "Marriott wants to add 30,000 rooms this year. We will add that in the next 2 weeks." When you have a marginal cost of zero, you can grow exponentially for much, much less capital. That's one of the great advantages of the times we're living in today.

Most people live in what I call an **analog fabrication**. This world requires a lot of capital and natural resources even to get started. Whereas when you're operating in the world of programming digital information, you can get infinite distribution for one production fee.

When you have a marginal cost of zero, you can grow exponentially for much, much less capital.

This is where you need to understand that an organization's linear hierarchy usually develops in a traditional management model, whether deliberately or by unconscious design. In a traditional linear hierarchy, there is an inflexibility of process. The company usually owns a lot of assets, and its innovation is slow and incremental. And leadership decisions are almost always based on the past. How can you keep up with the pace of the world today using a model like this? How much money and time will a linear hierarchy organization have to spend to move such a large, stupid system into a phase of exponential growth? Using this model, it's impossible to build, much less scale, a company. Major decisions must be made at warp speed in order to pivot, adapt to, and stay ahead of a constant stream of market-altering disruptions that can completely fuck you and your business in a matter of days unless you're able to move your company out of harm's way and respond to the threat extremely quickly. You *cannot* do that in a traditional linear hierarchy. There is just too much bureaucracy and too many slow, outdated, dusty parts to put into gear.

When you work in the NOMEG model, the structure becomes neural rather than hierarchal. You pursue a massive purpose; you don't need many assets giving you incredible asset leverage; experimentation is natural and constant; and you work through digital communities that provide real-time results and feedback.

Today we understand the power of exponential growth of technology. The NOMEG model applies that same understanding and vision to grow organizations. The challenge is in how to use the vision of technology's exponential growth pattern and apply it in the functions of a growing company. Even though organizations have ideas that inspire growth, companies often operate with a human-like behavior. Compared to computers, humans are slow and prone to mistakes. For example, a typical sales process has four stages, each one with a person or team of people responsible for doing the work of their respective stage: prospecting, qualifying, following up, and closing. If one person or stage is failing, then the entire sales process fails. As long as there are humans in the system, growth will be slower and the organization will be at a greater risk for failure. Technology can help. Even if a company provides a human service or needs humans involved in its processes, it needs to integrate technology into its model to accelerate and improve the work of humans.

The Five Exponentials: Five Key Areas to Develop for Exponential Growth

| RELEVANCE | OMNIPRESENCE | TRUST | INTIMACY | CONTINUITY |

1 EXPONENTIAL CONTENT
How to multiply content created

2 EXPONENTIAL REACH
How to amplify the scope

3 EXPONENTIAL DIGITAL TRUST
How to build trust without human contact

4 EXPONENTIAL SALES (CONVERSATION)
How to close sales without humans

5 EXPONENTIAL DIGITAL RELATIONSHIPS
How to maintain effective relationships without contact

The NOMEG model defines five areas of work that can be enhanced by the use of technology in what I call the **five exponentials**: exponential content, exponential reach, exponential trust, exponential sales or conversion, and exponential digital relationships. This is a process in which every possible job in each area becomes digitized. Essentially, we're creating a production line, where you can see every part of the process. And every part is enabled by technology, which creates the capacity for exponential growth in every area of the process. With a digitized process, you should be able to grow each area of work exponentially every year.

It doesn't matter whether your company is a technology business or not; this model can and should be used in every organization, regardless of whether it has a business interest in the technology sector. Including the exponential growth mindset and the exponential growth process into the company equation is a must for every organization that wants to compete at a high level in the future.

You may be wondering whether the job of integrating technology into the company's processes is the responsibility of individual business units or the responsibility of the company. That job is a corporate responsibility, specifically the responsibility of the chief marketing officer (CMO). I classify anything related to improving your brand and the effectiveness of your brand's reach as the responsibility of the CMO. In that sense, incorporating the right technology to enhance the company's brand, strengthen consumer trust, improve sales, and expand the brand's reach falls to the duties of the CMO. I am currently using two different systems to implement the five exponentials in all my business units. One system employs a central staff that will handle the marketing and technology needs of the five exponentials, which business unit leaders can hire for a fee when they need it. The other system uses a small marketing team within each business unit. Each system has its advantages and disadvantages, but smaller business units tend to benefit from contracting with the central team when needed, as it affords them greater flexibility in their payroll expenses as well as fewer staff management responsibilities.

Before we dive into the details for each of the five exponentials, you need to know how to determine if you've achieved exponential growth. The way to find out is very simple: if you can increase your output by ten times with no more people, then you're in an exponential model.

Exponential content is the first phase of generating exponential growth. Before speaking about products and services, a marketing campaign needs to define whom the company is made for. You need to think about your company's "tribe," meaning whom you want to work for in the market and whom you want to make sure feels a sense of belonging to your company when you're building a community. Exponential growth comes from the markets, hence why marketing is so important here. The market needs to create that growth for you, and the only way it's going to do that is if you find your tribe within the market and make them want to be tied to your company. Creating a community and building the connection it has with your company is the purpose of your content.

The way I think about these tribes is based on a concept of the writer Andrew Solomon, who described the ability to connect to those with shared interests as **horizontal**

identity. Solomon defines horizontal identity as either an inherent or acquired trait that is generated through choices. He compares this to **vertical identity**, which he defines as traits that people get without a choice (e.g., race, gender, language, etc.). Exponential content is concerned with horizontal identities. For example, so-called "pet parents," who literally treat their pets like their children, would be your tribe if you were in the business of selling gourmet pet food, clothing, and the like. If you find or create places for them to gather, either digitally or physically (e.g., pet-friendly bars and cafes, retail shops, etc.), then obviously it's easier to reach them when you have a product or service for pet-loving people.

Exponential content operates along a scale that I call the **V3 system**. This system uses three stages to guide what kind of content we create. V1 is **viral**; V2 is **value**; and V3 is **sales**. We progressively interchange the content we put out according to the needs of the business. If we want to gain more exposure, we try to create content that can get traction on social media. If we want to build more trust with our tribe, then we produce content that is helpful and useful to them so they will follow you. And, of course, we must produce V3 content to drive revenue for the company, meaning we must effectively find ways to monetize the community. If you have too much of any one type of content, you will not have success. Too much V1 content might get you a lot of exposure, but you won't be able to retain that interest without V2 content. If you put out a lot of V2 content, then you may gain a strong and dedicated following, but without adding V3 content into the mix, you're going to have a hard time making any money for the business. If you have too much V3 content, however, then you're going to see a lot of churning in your tribe because people don't want to follow a person or brand that's only producing content to try to sell them something. The more quality V1, V2, and V3 content you feed your tribe, the more the community will grow.

Exponential reach is exponentially increasing the size of your tribe over a given period. It's created by adding up three sources of traffic:

1. Traffic you generate through your content.

2. Traffic you pay for.

3. Traffic you win through collaborations.

Marketing in a digital world is a traffic game, and by keeping constant tabs on how much traffic each of these sources generates is the best way to determine your reach and the effectiveness of each strategy. Regularly interchanging each of these traffic sources is how you can dominate the algorithms and create exponential reach.

Exponential trust is the precursor to sales. Before you can sell something to someone, you need to earn their trust first. How do you know whether you're getting your tribe's trust? By analyzing the four types of digital sales. Instead of thinking of sales as just one thing (i.e., closing a deal and generating revenue), I think of sales as four stages of trust. The first "sale" you have to make is getting people to follow you. If they don't follow you or don't want to follow you, then you're not selling. Getting people to follow you should be the easiest sale to make because it's *free*! The second sales stage is getting followers to commit to a database. If you are growing a company inside of Facebook, for example, then you are working to feed Facebook's platform by bringing people onto it or by helping to keep them there. You cannot get too dependent on any one platform, otherwise you may end up losing revenue if that platform changes something that negatively impacts your presence there. Build your own database outside of another company by getting followers to submit a way to contact them directly (e.g., email, phone, text, etc.). The third sales stage is generating explicit interest in one or more of your products or services. Once you know that someone has an explicit interest in something you're trying to sell, then they become a lead. The fourth stage of sales is simply to sell that lead, which should be easy to do by the time someone gets to the fourth stage.

> **The first "sale" you have to make is getting people to follow you.**

To build trust and generate **exponential sales and conversions**, you need intimacy. I'm not talking about romance here. I'm talking about having deep knowledge and understanding of who your tribe is and what they want. You can study Google analytics or any marketing data that a media platform offers and use that information to create **lead magnets**, which are anything that provides a subtle way of determining whether someone has an interest in one of your products or services. You can do that with what I call a **trust key product**. This is a product or service that is small enough to sell easily but that will give you an opportunity to sell something larger at a later time. For example, if I want people to buy into my Mastermind group, I might first sell them one of my digital courses, which range in price from $50 to $200. That's much less than the $20,000 that my Mastermind memberships are currently worth.

Why do I want those small sales worth fifty bucks? Because I want to bring people into the community, show them the value of my products and services, and gain their trust to follow me further. It's what I call the **ladder of value**. First, you give them something for free. Then you give them a sample that they pay for and then offer them a more high-ticket product or service.

Sales and conversion are all about intimacy, and there are several ways to get it. In the digital world, the new sales process requires you to go through three stages before trying to close the sale. The first stage is **digital empathy**. People want to be helped before they buy. The next stage is **social**

proof. This applies to reviews you get online or from word of mouth. People need to know what those who bought your product or service thought about it before they commit to a sale themselves. The final stage is **differentiation**. As well as quality and usefulness, people are drawn to the uniqueness of a product or service. They want to buy things that stand out from their respective competition.

Once you move through each of the stages of both intimacy and sales, you will be able to actually build **exponential digital relationships**. These are the relationships you want most of all, as they are the bedrock of the tribe and provide the foundation to expand the company's community exponentially. These are not passing transactions of one-off sales to random people but rather the establishment of opportunities for long-term revenue, such as subscriptions or memberships. Relationships produce long-term revenue, which in turn, provides most of the continuity you need to achieve to maintain exponential growth.

This may sound like a lot of work, but it's actually quite easy because all the data you need is automatically generated for you on social media platforms. Robots and algorithms do most of the work; it's just your job to understand how they work and then move people through the pipeline accordingly. Just remember that exponential growth in the digital world requires four things: **relevancy, omnipresence, intimacy**, and **continuity**.

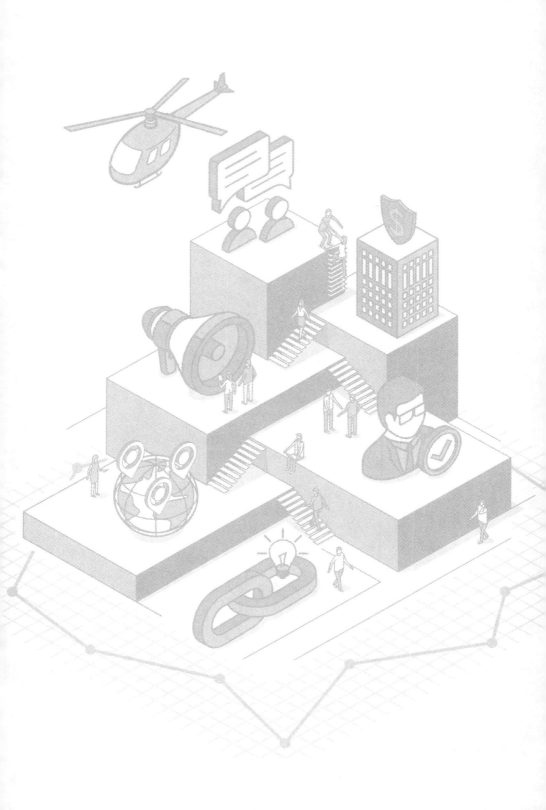

CHAPTER FIVE

FROM LOCAL TO GLOBAL

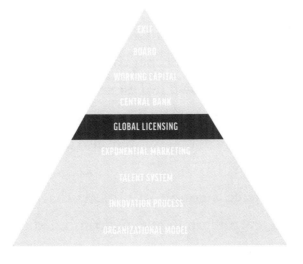

A definite part of the success of the NOMEG model has been its ability to demonstrate that you can achieve international growth—even without capital from the founders. This is obviously the Holy Grail for any entrepreneur, but I did not achieve it overnight. Actually, the formula the NOMEG system incorporates came about from one of the darkest financial times I had to face. This is that story.

With 4S Group's expansion of services, we began to scale up at an increasingly faster rate as projects and clients grew in both number and in the scope of services being sold. While we were still operating as a consultancy, we were not just doing market research anymore. We were now offering a wide range of services, dipping our toes into design, financial services, digital services, marketing and sales, and liaison services for construction and legal needs. In other words, we were growing into a full-service real estate development consultancy group. We could offer all those services because we knew the game that our clients were playing or wanting to play. Because of that confidence and growth, we decided to expand our own real estate development portfolio by buying, developing, and selling our own properties. The problem, however, was that we were also gambling with a lot more money.

We completed a couple of projects that did very well, generating a few million in revenue combined. That success spurred us to attempt our biggest project at the time: a twelve-story building in the emerging market of Veracruz, Mexico, which was comprised of around one hundred apartments. We got the loan from the bank, hired the architect, secured the land and the permits, and began what we planned to be several months' worth of construction.

Everything began perfectly. However, a few months into the project, while finishing the fourth floor, a double murder occurred right outside the building. Some things you just can't plan for or mitigate your risk around, and that's exactly the position in which we found ourselves at the time. The negative attention on the area scared away a lot of prospective buyers and left my partners and me with a pivotal decision: terminate the project and lose about two million dollars or finish the project with bank money and hope that things would turn around for the better in the coming months. We ended up going through with the latter, but when the project was finished, we could not sell any of the units.

The bank will not feel sorry for you in such a situation, of course. They still want the money they loaned you as well as the 12-plus percent interest it was accumulating at the agreed-upon time of repayment (remember, these are Latin American interest rates). That put us in a dire situation because we were now millions of dollars in debt, with no incoming revenue to pay back the loan. Though we all had some savings, it was not enough to pay the debt. This was pivotal for 4S, as the profit we made from our consulting unit was only enough to pay the interest rate on this particular loan. Technically, we were bankrupt.

We needed an escape plan for that moment. Our dire financial situation led us to explore markets outside our own in an attempt to generate the additional revenue we needed to pay off the debt. My partners and I decided to use our Mexico profits to pay the interest and use the money we were getting from our international operations for the actual loan amount. The problem was that we were only getting a small amount of revenue from our international market. We had not invested much of our time or money into market operations outside Mexico. At the time, we mistakenly believed the traditional business view to be true: conquer your own town/state/region/country before expanding into new ones.

I decided to turn my focus to the international side of the business, mainly because we really needed that new cash flow. I was sick of scraping by while worrying that the next bit of misfortune would ruin the business and cause me to lose what little bit I had personally. I began traveling extensively to drive up our international revenues. The more I traveled and grew our international business, the more money I could bring home. The good news was that at that point, my first book had some international distribution and other Latin American markets were growing. We were digging the company out of debt. I opened offices in Guatemala, El Salvador, Costa Rica, Panama, Colombia, Peru, and Argentina.

When you're doing the kind of consulting work I was doing, the problem is not making sales but rather going back and actually completing the project you sold. After a few years of constant travel and temporarily living around Latin America and beyond, I was getting close to burnout. While our strategy was proving successful, I knew the model was not sustainable and began to look for other solutions.

Fortunately, I had met another consultant during my travels who helped large accounting companies open new offices and create partnerships in other countries. He assisted us with devising a system that could help us scale internationally, and although the ideas he gave us were not the ones we ultimately used to grow internationally, he provided us with the kick-start to a global mindset around business.

But What about Investment?

Growing internationally requires capital at some point. You may need to expand your inventory, your team, your facilities, etc., but if the owners don't have to put down money, where does the investment come from?

We settled on two primary strategies to secure capital and fund territorial expansion, which work just as well when expanding not only to different countries but also to different cities, states, regions, etc. The first tool we used is called **licensing**, and the other is commonly referred to as **private debt**.

In business, licensing is the act of allowing a third party to use the products, services, materials, brand name and/or image, or any other property owned by a company. There are countless ways a licensing agreement can function, but it's generally an agreement between the third party and the owner of the property that allows the third party to sell the owner's property in exchange for a royalty fee and/or a share of any revenues generated by the use of said property.

The other tool, private debt, simply refers to any form of debt accrued by a private business, whether that debt comes from the use of a bank loan, credit, private investors, or even through the surrender of company equity in exchange for cash.

That's the short explanation of these growth tools, but since they're so important to the NOMEG model, we need to dig deeper into what they mean and how they work. We'll talk more extensively about private debt in the upcoming finance chapter, but for now let's explore the concept of licensing on its own.

LICENSING

Operating international offices so far away is complicated and costly. If you are growing, it is hard to sustain the fixed costs that these offices create. If you remember the matrix we spoke about, we mentioned the Napoleonic chain. We need entrepreneurs that connect with our vision but are physically in the specific territories we want to grow in. It's important to mention here that we are looking to sell in the markets we go into; we are not there to outsource labor.

To handle that growth, you need a legal structure light enough that it does not generate fixed costs but legally binding to ensure responsibility from the local staff. For the NOMEG system, that answer is licensing.

Remember that licensing is when a company allows a third party to use its products, services, materials, branding, or any other property it owns. Licensing is not a new concept although it has not necessarily been used the way the NOMEG system uses it. Under NOMEG, licensees are actually leaders of the organization, meaning they are **intrapreneurs** (i.e., someone who acts like an entrepreneur but who works within an organization) focused on geographical growth. In most cases where licensing is used, the licensee is not considered part of the organization. A traditional licensing agreement allows a licensee to use patented property, produce and sell goods/services, and/or use a brand name or trademark. In return, the licensee

Under NOMEG, licensees are actually leaders of the organization.

must agree to various conditions regarding the use of the licensor's property and will most likely have to make royalty payments back to the licensor.

In the NOMEG model, however, licensees are acting as actual parts of the whole organization. We spoke about how NOMEG organizations are a kind of "orchestra of entrepreneurs," and in a geographical sense, they are bound to the organization through licensing. The NOMEG licensee is part of a revenue-sharing program with the organization, which allows the licensee more freedom to produce, market, and sell products and services as well as operate their regional outfit however they wish. The goal of a licensing agreement in the NOMEG model is to find a licensee who (a) knows their market very well and (b) is capable of managing a business. If the licensee has those abilities, then both the organization and the licensee can form a mutually beneficial relationship.

The other thing to understand about licensing is that its definition is often misinterpreted because people often confuse licensing with franchising. When you have a franchise, you act as an independent owner of a branch from a corporation's brand. The franchise model is designed to clone a business. When you walk into a McDonald's restaurant anywhere in the world, though it may be owned by a franchisee, it will look and operate the same as every other McDonald's. There's nothing wrong with that model, but when you're a growing company in a capital-scarce scenario, you cannot be as aggressive in terms of standardization.

Licensing, like franchising, helps you scale a business service or product offering in a particular location by incorporating other options, but unlike franchising, licensing isn't as strict in terms of cloning the business. Because things like wealth, culture, demographics, and general market interest vary by region, the ability to tailor a business strategy to a specific market is incredibly important when both creating and scaling a business. Licensing affords you greater control of that tailoring process as well as your cash flow. Let me explain what I mean with an example.

BUILDING THE LICENSING STRUCTURE

Imagine that I want to expand into a new country—let's say Peru—but I'm not doing business there at the time and I don't have any money to move into the territory. The first thing I want to find is what I call a **regional representative**, which is someone who will be responsible for the operations and revenue of a particular region, using the goods, services, and/or brand offered by the main business entity (i.e., the company that legally owns, produces, sponsors, and/or is responsible for the products and services offered).

Appointing a representative in the NOMEG model is based on two criteria: whether we believe they have the talent to become one of our partners and whether they win more business regardless of their partnership. We need time to get to know a regional representative, to see whether they are actually the right fit with us. We do that by allowing reps to sell whatever product or service we offer for one year. For example, if I were manufacturing pens, the rep could sell pens in, say, Peru. If I'm doing consulting work, then the rep could sell consulting services in Peru or whatever territory they prefer. The rep would only get a percentage of the sales they made because they are only selling the company's products and services and do not have to pay any of the costs, such as production, distribution, branding, legal, etc.

Usually when you're selling in a new territory that is far away from your main office, the sales are not going to be the most profitable, but that's okay. This stage is used to get to know the representative and assess the feasibility of a potential partnership with them. The regional rep does not get a salary, working instead as an independent contractor who is paid through a sales commission. Before you settle on a sales percentage for the regional rep, you must decide what amount of revenue you need to get out of that particular office to cover operating costs. Do not expect to win money in the first sales period with your regional teams. Look at them instead as test pilots, serving the purpose of exploring the profitability of new markets, products, services, and/or sales and marketing strategies.

Let's imagine that your new regional representative does well in their role, consistently meeting or exceeding the sales goals for their territory and generating a high amount of revenue for the company over a six- to twelve-month period. At that point, you may begin weighing the option of promoting them to the position of regional partner, which is where licensing comes into play.

It's important to keep in mind that a regional representative in this context is not the same as a sales rep in a given territory. The regional representative is responsible for running their office just as they would if they were its owner. They are given a budget for periods of either six or twelve months, and with that budget, they are responsible for generating a specified amount of revenue within their region. Because this role requires a considerable amount more responsibility than your standard sales rep, I only appoint people to the position of regional representative who my partners and I believe have the potential to become a partner. I tell every regional representative of that intention, giving them additional incentive to perform well in the regional representative role. The regional representative, in other words, is a milestone position and a pathway to the more lucrative, more autonomous position of regional partner.

SPLITTING THE REVENUES BETWEEN REGIONAL PARTNERS AND THE COMPANY

So what is a regional partner, exactly? First of all, a regional partner has to create a company. As a regional representative, a partner will have met or exceeded their region's revenue goals without going over their budget for at least one year. Revenue goals vary by region, accounting for the region's size, population, economics, brand presence, and other factors. How long a regional rep remains in that position before being promoted to regional partner also varies, depending on such factors as the amount of revenue generated, the percentage of the budget spent, the consistency with which goals are met, and more.

Once a regional rep has shown that they would be a good partner for the company, it is time for them to start their own company. The company created by the partner will then sign a licensing contract with your company, forming a relationship between two independent companies bounded by a licensing contract that clearly defines the sales splits between your company and the regional partner. You must be very careful when deciding on what the split will be (e.g., 50/50, 80/20, 70/30, etc.). Every split should be based on a case-by-case analysis.

Your company will serve as the corporation in the deal, placing the partner's company in charge of selling the corporation's products and services, with the money going into the corporate account. The regional partner does not touch the money, allowing the corporation (i.e., your company) to control the cash flow. Let's look at a simple example to illustrate this arrangement.

Imagine that you own a company that makes a specific type of pants, which you have patented or otherwise hold an exclusive license to. Your regional partner sets up a storefront that sells these pants. In one week, that partner sells $1,000 worth of pants. The first thing you want to do is take your royalty fee out of that gross profit. Let's say that the royalty agreement is 10 percent, so you take out $100 from the

$1,000 in sales. Now you're left with $900 in gross revenue, which you would then split among what the regional partner gets and what the corporation gets. If the corporation and the partner have a typical product split of 80/20, then $180 goes to the partner and the other $720 goes to the corporation. The partner then uses that money however they like. They will pay themselves, hire whomever they want to hire, style their office or store however they like, and make all their own marketing and sales strategy decisions without interference from the corporation. That's the primary difference between licensing and franchising. Licensees hold the license to represent the brand exclusively in a particular territory, and they have complete control to manage their operation however they wish.

THE MONEY QUESTION

A common question that comes to mind regarding licensing agreements is how to determine the revenue split between the corporate entity and the regional partner. The first step is to look at what each party is doing to create revenue. How much is the partner paying to operate their company (e.g., rent, utilities, labor, advertising, taxes and fees, maintenance expenses, etc.)? How much is the corporation spending to produce, advertise, and distribute the products and services being offered? How much is a specific product or service's license worth (i.e., what is the value of the brand)? Every service or product should have a specific split, so the percentages shared among both companies will change from product to product or service to service. Products, for example, usually have a much lower profit margin than services, so the royalty fee on products is often lower. That's because you do not want to make it unnecessarily difficult for regional partners to turn a profit for themselves. The idea is to create a mutually beneficial partnership with one another.

Royalty percentages are also subject to the industry and to brand strength. Every product or service has its own splinters, so to speak, so it's very important that companies study the cost structure and decide what amount is necessary to fulfill each product or service specifically. If you're operating a clothing brand, for instance, you do not want to use a royalty and profit split figure that applies universally to all your products. Once you understand the fulfillment costs, that's when you define the royalty percentage and gross profit split.

Services are a little different than products, in that they usually require a higher split for the regional partner (typically a 70/30 split). Imagine that the corporation is selling branded events. We, meaning the corporation, have conducted a couple market studies and decided that our events (e.g., speaking engagements, business expos, product releases, sporting or fitness events, etc.) would do well in a specific region. With many event services, almost all the work is done locally (e.g., securing the location, facilities, and permits; setting up and breaking down necessary features, such as stages, chairs, tables, etc.; hiring local staff; and more). This additional work performed locally by the regional partner tends to warrant the higher split for the regional partner (vis-à-vis in the case of products). Also, for high-cost services (and products), you really need a local representative to facilitate sales.

People often think that you do not need a local sales presence in our digital age, since you can sell your products and services online. This is not true of big-ticket items, though. You may be able to do well selling tickets online for an event that costs less than, say, $1,000 to attend. But if you're selling an event whose tickets cost several thousand dollars, for example, then it's much harder to get people to pull the trigger on such a large purchase from a website. You need someone on the ground who can personally sell the customer on the experience and take the time to show the customer exactly what their money is buying. Think about it like this: Are you more likely to buy a new car through a purely digital process or from an individual or company after seeing the actual

You need someone on the ground who can personally sell the customer on the experience and take the time to show the customer exactly what their money is buying.

car in person and getting to test drive it? This is the benefit of having a local partner.

As noted above, because your regional partner has to do most of the work and maybe even cover some of the up-front costs to generate these local sales, they will need to be compensated with a higher percentage of sales, sometimes as much as 70 percent or more of the split.

DIGITAL TRAFFIC PARTNERS

Just because local, on-the-ground regional partners are useful in the NOMEG model, they are by no means the only type of partner suited to this system. Some companies have a sales structure that does not require a local physical presence. As an example, let's think of an e-commerce site. You can handle sales from a corporate office and launch logistics from that central location.

The important thing about the NOMEG model is not the fact that there are regional partners but the fact that you have actual intrapreneurs working on sales and geographic reach. In those cases, what should you do? We coined the term **digital traffic partners** to refer to these agreements where location is not necessarily important but the actual territory is. These digital traffic partners are tasked with building up the company brand and driving sales in a particular region either exclusively or primarily through the use of digital tools like social media, online advertising, surveys, email marketing, and more.

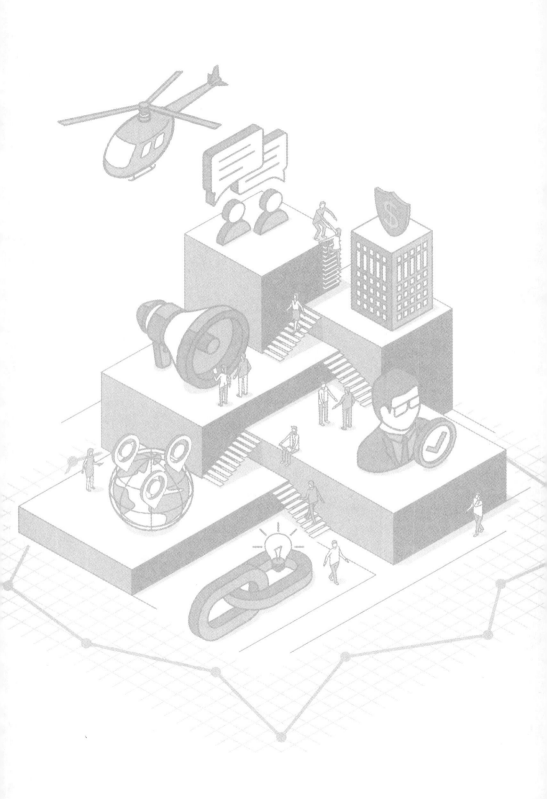

FINANCE IN THE NOMEG SYSTEM

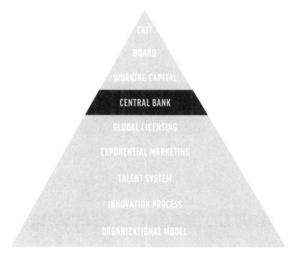

At the heart of financial management in the NOMEG Model is what I call the **central bank**.

When I first began to build the model, I quickly understood that it uses an organizational model based on SBUs that basically divides a company into autonomous cells. While the model emphasizes segregation in operations, it centralizes the complete financial function. This means that a central bank is created for the complete chain that reports directly to the CEO.

It is important to remember that NOMEG was created for managing *profitable* companies, so financial function is key to **preserve cash** and amplify the company through **leverage**.

Let's take a brief look, from a bird's-eye view, of the responsibilities of the central bank before we examine them in greater detail. At its core, the central bank has two main concerns:

1. preserving cash and creating leverage through cash flow,

2. and creating inorganic growth through alternative capital.

Central Bank Duties for Preserving Cash

We have structured the chapter as follows:

1. Making sure the numbers are correct for all business units and the company at large (e.g., profits and losses, assets and liabilities, taxes, etc.)

2. Selecting correct financial projections

3. Protecting against fraud (from both inside and outside the organization)

4. Improving overall fiscal decisions

The first function of the central bank is basic **bookkeeping** responsibilities. The staff reviews and ensures the correctness of not only the company's finances but also the financial numbers of its business units and partnerships (for both regional and digital traffic partners).

When you have a large number of regional partners, digital traffic partners, and business unit leaders, the main problem is that you have to keep everyone on the same page in terms of profits/losses from each of these regions and business units. The central bank acts as a treasury in this way, creating financial reports for every business unit and partnership to provide the company greater transparency into their operations while also managing the company's overall fiscal positions. This means the central bank controls the company's cash, services its debts, oversees its taxation strategies, and researches and executes investment opportunities.

It may sound as though the central bank would need an army to juggle all these duties, but with the help of technology, strong talent, and plenty of trials and errors to find the perfect formula, my central bank handles all these responsibilities both for my companies and for their respective units and partnerships with a staff of just fourteen people.

Reporting the revenue and profits from each region and business unit to their respective partners and leaders is key to the model's success. If the central bank is not fully transparent, accessible, and consistent with a standardized reporting process, seeds of distrust and friction will surely be planted throughout the company. This is why it's critical that the central bank be accessible and that the department prioritize transparency with every partner and business unit leader, providing them with information, assistance, and reports as timely and regularly as possible.

The second function of the central bank is **forecasting** financial developments for the regional partners, the business units, and the company itself. In finance, you have to think about the future at all times. That's the basis for making projections and forecasting economic trends. With the central bank and the financial information for your company, its business units, and any of its partnerships, it's fairly easy to predict trends in different regions and services. The central bank is plugged into each business unit and region online, allowing it to access up-to-date information on how well the trends are going for each business unit and region. Having information on the operations of all the company's units and regions enables the central bank to forecast trends, dissipate revenue, and project profits quickly and efficiently. That analytical power, in addition to the transparency that a central bank offers, is a great asset to your partners and business unit leaders as well.

The company's central bank handles projections the same way an equity investor or traditional bank would: analyze the business potential of every idea and operation.

To do that, the central bank studies a wide range of factors, including the total addressable market size, the expertise of the operators, the profit margins, the size of any debt that would be incurred by the company, and the possibility of losing your capital or your enterprise completely. In other words, the central bank executes due diligence on every partner and business unit as though it were considering buying the business. Instead of buying it, of course, the central bank reports its findings to the company leaders (i.e., the COO, CEO, and the board) so they can better prepare a course of action regarding individual units and partners as well as market trends and general financial decisions.

Another important feature of a central bank is its protections against fraud. If individual business units had complete control of their finances, there would be greater risk for a leader to cook the books, so to speak. Remember that business unit leaders earn a percentage of their unit's profit share, so making their unit appear more profitable on paper than it really is could be a tempting prospect for them to make more money than they deserve. We combat that temptation by issuing business unit leaders—as well as regional and digital traffic partners—phantom stocks in the company. As an added safeguard, the NOMEG model ensures that all central bank members are salary-based employees of the company. By doing so, central bank members have no financial interest in how much a business unit makes or doesn't make.

Finding ways to generate revenue without giving up any equity in the company is a little trickier because there are several ways to do it. Some tools for securing capital, such as high-interest loans, will get you into more trouble than they're worth, while others are often overlooked in the venture capital model. It's important to explain what I mean in detail, so let's save the specifics of finding and using capital for the next chapter.

Inorganic Growth through Capital

All the objectives for preserving cash are not new or radical. What is radical is the second set of objectives, which form two of the central bank's pillars of responsibilities:

1. Managing the mergers and/or acquisitions of other companies. (Note that mergers between NOMEG and non-NOMEG companies are rare, as a traditional business model cannot easily synchronize with the NOMEG model and vice versa.)

2. Gaining leverage without giving up equity. (We will explore the concept of private risk-carrying debt in the following chapter.)

Although it's a stage we typically associate with very large companies, one of the most important ways for the central bank to secure capital is its involvement in **mergers and acquisitions (M&A)**. Remember that in the NOMEG model, the CEO's job is to create the talent machine and supervise the central bank, but perhaps most importantly, it is their job to find new ideas and growth opportunities for the company (e.g., business innovations, mergers, acquisitions, etc.). Part of that search includes acquisitions, of course, meaning they work closely with the central bank since it is the entity overseeing all the financial arrangements needed to buy another company. It's important to reiterate here that NOMEG companies do not usually merge with non-NOMEG companies, simply because the model is still too rarely used. To merge with a non-NOMEG company would require a significant buy-in from the organization because it would have to change much, if not all, of its operations model. That said, it is by no means out of the realm of possibility for NOMEG and non-NOMEG companies to merge. If the companies in question can synchronize how they wish to operate and manage themselves well enough, then a merger is certainly

> One of the most important ways for the central bank to secure capital is its involvement in mergers and acquisitions (M&A).

possible. For our purposes here, however, let's focus on the central bank's role in acquisitions.

Eventually, the NOMEG model, like all business models, will reach a certain level where growth opportunities are limited. Incremental growth is simply harder and slower at a certain point when only using the same strategies that have allowed you to scale in the past. When that happens, you must again adapt and innovate, and the NOMEG model provides the room and options to do just that, no matter how large the company becomes. To keep growing beyond your limits, you have to focus your vision on both the inner workings of the company and the outward opportunities in your midst simultaneously. Mergers and acquisitions offer an opportunity to expand into new markets as well as the current markets in which the company may be involved. But the goal is not to expand aimlessly by acquiring or merging with any company in any industry.

Mergers and acquisitions should be designed to strengthen the company's existing operations as well as its prospects for adding new markets, industries, and/or businesses to its portfolio. What does that mean? It means that to keep growing the company, you have to make strategic acquisition and/or merger decisions with competitors, supply chains, or other entities that bolster not only continued revenue growth but also efficiencies and synergies in the processes and overall structure of the company. With M&As

you should be looking for new revenue streams *and* ways to make your existing streams more profitable. Sometimes you may have to settle for one or the other, but the goal is to get both from a merger or acquisition.

Again, a NOMEG CEO is always looking for a great new idea, and sometimes that great new idea exists in another company. We tend to think of mergers and acquisitions as something that huge corporations do with one another. You may envision a bunch of people in black and gray suits sitting in a conference room somewhere near Wall Street discussing how their huge company can buy or join some other huge company. Sure, that happens, but it's not exclusive to massive corporations with billions of dollars to throw at each other. Most companies, including mine, do not have huge amounts of capital lying around to buy out their competitors whenever they want. Still, the majority of mergers and acquisitions occur among small- to medium-sized businesses through cleverly structured deals even though they're likely not as comfortable with the terminology as the corporate juggernauts out there.

NOMEG companies approach M&As the same way that they would approach adding a new business unit to the company. Like adding business units, the key to the success of an acquisition or merger is synergy. Does the company you're looking to acquire or merge with add value to your existing business? Will your business add value to the company in question, and if so, how much? If both companies complement each other well, fill in each other's gaps, and strengthen each other's weaknesses, then you can achieve explosive growth in both companies by combining the two.

Imagine for a moment that you have a company selling an average of $100,000 in products and services per year. You find another company selling the same or similar types of products and services but only at 10 percent ($10,000) of your company's total sales, yet the projections tell you that they will do $11,000 in sales the following year and $12,000 the year after that. With your company's infrastructure, client base, and industry knowledge, you predict that you can take this other company to $20,000 in sales within two years. This is a prime target for the type of company that you want to buy: you can take it to the next level without much additional financial expense due to your existing operations system and lines of business. In other words, you want to find more ways to capitalize on the work and money you put in. You can make them an offer based on their own valuation of $12,000 in sales within two years, but you're looking at it from a much larger growth rate (here, $20,000), due to the notion that you will connect that company to your company.

The objective of a merger or acquisition is to structure a deal in which your company's assets (i.e., cash, facilities, talent, industry knowledge, loan threshold, etc.) can accelerate the profits of another company. You should have an equation, of sorts, for how much it will cost to acquire the other company so you can determine when you expect to turn a profit and how much of a profit it will be. For instance, a great deal is generally understood as one that takes less than five years to recuperate what you spent to acquire the company. For instance, you may offer enough cash to compensate for the company's own projections of short-term growth (e.g., two to five years) but not so much that you'll get burned if the company doesn't grow past that mark.

Once you create the growth you're looking for, then you can start "paying" your company with the profits. The synergy between your company and the company you acquired or merged with pays for any M&A expenses, and ideally, it will bring in more revenue for the company as a whole. In the end, you are only adding another link to the company's chain of business streams, but you must be sure that it's a strong link.

That may sound complicated, but it's actually simple when you look at the numbers. For example, I usually buy 10 percent of the company that I want to go into, a minority percentage. Then I tell the company's leader(s) that I want an option to buy a majority stake in the company if I do X growth and X payments. If I can reach those marks, then by the end of the deal, I will own a majority stake in that company. I could then use the same process to buy out more of the company in another multiyear deal. If the company agrees and I'm able to reach those expectations, then I could either stay on as a business leader with your typical percentages or I could hire someone else to manage that division. If the company doesn't reach the profitability rate that I want (let's say 50 percent profit over the costs) within a certain amount of time, then I can sell my share, extract my portion of the profits, and use them to try again somewhere else.

The only way to invest wisely is to know the future of the company as well as possible. You should avoid injecting your own money into a company until you have robust and reliable research on its growth projections.

> **The only way to invest wisely is to know the future of the company as well as possible.**

An added bonus of buying shares of other companies is that it affords you more exit options from your own company as well, should you need them. No matter how well your company may be doing now or how strong its growth projections are, every leader must have an exit strategy planned. Exiting a company is not simply jumping ship when the seas get rough, either. Oftentimes an entrepreneur or CEO exits their company to actually help the business grow and/or improve, making the need for a leader's exit path even more critical to the success of both the leader and the company itself.

There are more ways for the central bank to generate capital, of course. Let's take a glance at the basic methods for gaining capital without losing equity in your company.

In 2020, I had the opportunity to interview several founders who received very large exits from their companies. I was surprised that by the time the company had grown, the founders sometimes controlled less than 10 percent of the equity. They had done the work, but they ultimately gave away the upside of their company for the sake of immediate injections of capital from investors.

Critics will say that growth sucks cash and if you are not providing cash for growth, then you are not growing as fast as you could grow. That argument leaves you with a new question: How can I provide cash for growing the company without giving up equity?

Conventional management models tend to think of the finance department as an administrative function, handling basic accounting needs like tax preparation and payroll and simply reporting what a company has profited and lost over a particular period of time. NOMEG's central bank is much more than that. The central bank is responsible for the fiscal strategies of the entire company. This is an important distinction to make, due to the level of autonomy among business units in the NOMEG model. Because business unit leaders have so much control over their units, it could lead to a bad use of their economic resources if they didn't have finance experts overseeing their fiscal decisions. That is, in short, the purpose of the central bank: to control all the money from the business units, create fiscal strategies for the entire company, and provide financial advice to the company.

It could sound restrictive, but this idea is anything but. While protecting the company from bad investments, I also allow the unit leaders to be creative without the added weight of numbers and finances. In this way, they can think of projects first and foremost. They can be wildly creative and then get a reality check (if needed) through the oversight of the central bank. It is better to create when there are no limits to the imagination, and the NOMEG model provides a structure that can support that degree of freedom.

The following chapter goes in depth into the strategies for acquiring alternative working capital that can help accelerate growth for a company (without giving up equity!).

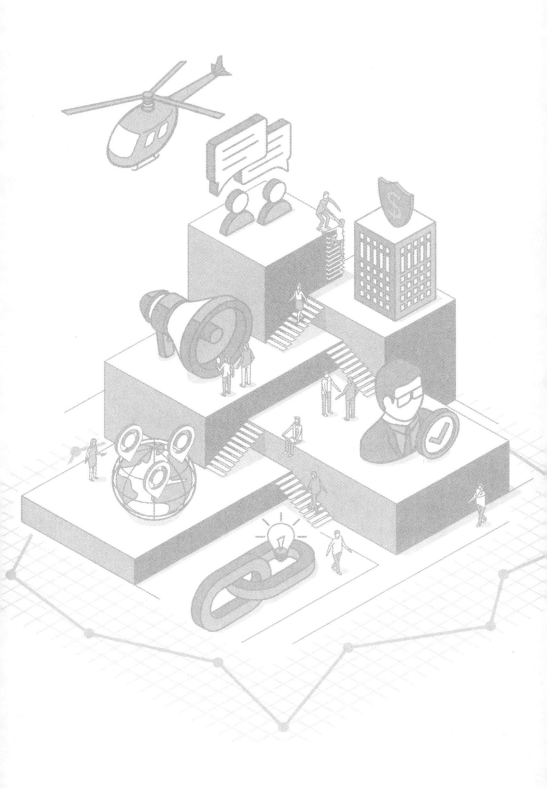

CHAPTER SEVEN

WORKING CAPITAL

To scale your business, you will need some form of capital to bankroll the expansion costs. The easiest way to fund your expansion is through **investor equity**, meaning you sell a certain stake in your company to an outside investor(s). By selling off a portion of your company to investors, however, you are essentially chopping off an arm or a leg or both in exchange for a lump cash payment. Anytime you use someone else's money, the risk is the same because the cost is very high. What is the cost? The cost is that you inevitably lose control over your company, in an amount proportional to the percentage you sold off to investors.

If you borrow money from the bank, on the other hand, you don't give away any portion of your company. That doesn't mean there is no risk involved, however, as you are gambling on your company's ability to repay the loan with interest. If you can't repay the bank on time, then the bank can seize your assets, garner your income, or use another method to recover the loan. Throughout most of Latin America, a company cannot separate business and personal assets, either. To secure even a business loan, the company's owner must also put up their personal assets as collateral. If you do not have enough assets or income to cover your debt, then you could find yourself vulnerable to taking on higher-interest loans, being subject to foreclosures, and experiencing other repercussions that can wreak havoc on your finances. The burden is entirely on you to use the loan to increase your revenue enough so you can pay for both the costs of your expansion and the costs of the loan itself (i.e., interest, service fees, and principle), not to mention supporting your own personal expenses.

If you bring in money from investors and the company goes bankrupt, at least you won't be so susceptible to the financial challenges associated with debt. In that aspect, investor equity is certainly a less stressful type of raising cash for growth, but you are giving away a percentage of your company. The more money you seek from investors, the more control of the company you will be giving away.

Securing financing definitely taxes you, personally. You won't sleep as well knowing that you have less control of your company, nor will you sleep well knowing that you're in debt to a bank that will come for your assets and possessions if you cannot repay the loan within a specific time frame. Either way, when you take someone else's money, you will not sleep like a baby again until you can either pay the money back or buy back the equity stake you sold to outside investors.

There is a third tool you can use, which is commonly referred to as **convertible debt**. Though lesser known as a financing tool than equity shares or bank loans, convertible debt acts as a kind of hybrid between equity shares and loans but without the legal and asset risks of a traditional bank loan. Let's say that I need a hundred thousand dollars, but I either do not want to take out a bank

> **There is a third tool you can use, which is commonly referred to as convertible debt.**

loan or I am not eligible for a bank loan. I can go to an investor or group of investors and negotiate a convertible debt agreement, in which the investor(s) loan me cash under the terms that if I cannot repay the loan, then they get a percentage of my company. Convertible debt is still not a great deal, but depending on the terms of the loan, it can be a better option than a traditional bank loan or an up-front sale of equity. The deal is structured as debt, except that you are essentially putting a portion of your company up as collateral. If you fail to pay off the debt, then you will be forced to give up whatever amount of equity shares you and the investor(s) agreed to in the loan terms.

No matter what type of loan you take on as a company, you cannot avoid taking on private debt (i.e., debt held by a private company), which in turn, creates a financial risk to both your company and your personal assets. That's what is so appealing about being a regional partner: the reduced risk of running a company. The regional partner does not own any equity in the corporation, but they do get the benefit of selling products and services that already have a proven market value and brand recognition. On the other hand, the corporation is able to reduce some of their risk by using the regional partner's resources to drive growth in a new territory rather than footing the bill of opening another location, taking on more employees, launching a marketing campaign specific to the region, etc.

Regional partners also open up new options for debt negotiations, should the corporation need to borrow cash for growth needs. Suppose that I had a regional partner who was selling a lot of product and meeting all their revenue goals. The partner comes to me and asks for $100,000 to increase their sales even more. Maybe they want to open a second store or office, hire more people, purchase more equipment, or secure more inventory. If that region's market demand is growing and they're a good partner—meaning they are loyal and have proven their ability to turn my investments in their region into greater profit margins—then I may want to give them the $100,000 to feed that region's growth.

If I don't have $100,000, then I could ask to borrow it from an investor, either as a cash loan with interest or under convertible debt terms. The difference in taking on debt with regional partners in play, however, is that I can negotiate with investors to provide a cash return using the revenues generated by my regional partners rather than through my corporation. In other words, if the regional partner and my corporation agree to split the profits 80/20 or 70/30, I can bring in an investor and offer them a share of either the corporation's or the regional partner's profits. In the example given, I would negotiate with my regional partner to have them give up a portion of their profits in exchange for the $100,000 I gave to their operation. It's another tool for juggling capital to fund growth, while reducing the amount of risk you expose yourself to when taking on debt with unfavorable terms.

Perhaps more than any other financial aspect of business, finding a balance between capital and debt (or avoiding debt altogether) is the most critical part of scaling a company. Every company must grow to survive in the long term. That means the company will have to explore and conquer new markets. Conducting market research is great and certainly needed, but working with regional representatives and partners is the best way that I've found to actually test the profitability of those new markets. You give yourself greater control of maintaining that critical balance between capital and debt (aka assets and liabilities) by using regional partners to drive brand awareness and revenues rather than plunging the company into debt by taking on the full costs of expanding into new territories.

Finding a balance between capital and debt (or avoiding debt altogether), is the most critical part of scaling a company.

In Latin America, we don't have an operating environment to obtain a bunch of capital, due to large limitations in the venture capital ecosystem throughout the region. As a result, being an investor in Latin America is quite hard since you don't have exit events that help reduce risks if you invest in a small company. That's why we came out with this finance model for the NOMEG system, in which the investors deal in basically the same risk as a venture capitalist but with the financing written as a debt instead of equity. That allows the investor to deal very high returns in this mode but without the entrepreneur giving up a percentage of their business.

In financial terms, we are indexing the yield and principal payment to a royalty on the company's total revenue. In essence, the company pays back the investor in installments (taken from its overall revenue) over an agreed-upon period of time until the debt is paid off in full. The percentage of interest is usually variable, and the multiple depends on the time it takes the company to repay the investor.

This model may seem similar to a royalty agreement, but there are some stark differences. In a typical royalty agreement, you might get $100,000 from an investor who then wants $1 from every unit you sell for life. That means you have someone effectively draining cash out of your company, potentially well after you pay back that initial $100,000. In the NOMEG model, however, you're paying back the debt through your sales, and the amount you actually pay back depends on how quickly you can repay the debt.

To reiterate, the investor is at risk alongside the company to some degree. This model can also be used as a way to get investors to fund specific projects as opposed to investing in the whole company. With a contract in place that explains the mutual risk shared by the company and the investor, if the company does not sell the project that an investor put money into, then the company does not have to return any money to the investor. That's very different from the venture capital model, in that private debt is used for specific projects rather than for purchasing a portion of the company itself. So let's say I have a project to bring in a specific inventory of TVs, which is a project we analyzed and believe we can turn a healthy profit on through Amazon. Imagine that I wanted to bring in $500,000 worth of TVs, which I believe I can sell for a gross revenue of $800,000. I propose to give an investor 15 percent of the net profits (i.e., $120,000), and I will pay back the $500,000 over the next ten years. If the investor agrees, then as soon as the inventory begins to sell, I would provide regular (e.g., weekly, monthly, quarterly, etc.) payments to the investor. They know that their money is not tied to any other resources in the company, which creates a project-based investing style that many investors prefer.

From an investor's perspective, this is a model that offers more options and protections than a standard format of purchasing a chunk of a company and then hoping it's successful enough to generate a decent **return on investment (ROI)** at some point in time. Take the TV sales investment as an example. The investor owns that $500,000 worth of inventory and is going to recuperate their money one way or another on that deal even if that means finding someone else to sell the TVs. It's a good idea for the investor and the person they're investing in to have a thorough understanding of one another, how they do business, and what each other's expectations are as well as maintain regular communication. As the investor, you will have to ultimately take a leap of faith, so it's best to know where you're jumping from, who you're jumping with, and how far the fall may be. Personally, I often invest in people from my Mastermind group because I spend a lot of time with them and, as a result, I am afforded ample time and opportunities to understand both their ideas and who they are as individuals and entrepreneurs. It's not mandatory for someone to be personally familiar with an investor or for an investor to be personally familiar with a company or individual they are considering investing in, but it can't hurt, and it's certainly wise to know as much as possible prior to taking that mutual leap of faith.

NOMEG's financial model may have been born from the innovations needed to grow within the economic realities of Latin America, but that doesn't mean it's restricted to Latin America. It works just as well in the US; in fact, I believe it works better than the current venture capital model that Silicon Valley loves so much: (a) You don't have to give away your company to gain investors, (b) the investor gets a definitive return and has an exit available to them, and (c) the investor is part of the risk of the company and, therefore, more invested in making it a successful one.

The investor is further protected by the structure of financing a specific project, wherein the company provides a specified amount of cash flow returns to guarantee a minimum payment on the debt. Even though the investor is going after the cash flows of the project, the company can guarantee to service a minimum amount of the debt to create a minimum ROI for the investor. That offers the investor extra certainty that the minimum amount of debt is going to be acquired by the company, not just the project. The more options companies and investors have to reduce risks and liabilities, the easier it becomes to find a deal that benefits everyone, which in turn, facilitates more investment opportunities with less headache. That's the beauty of a system like this: it provides greater financial flexibility to companies in need of capital and more options and exit events for those interested in making an investment.

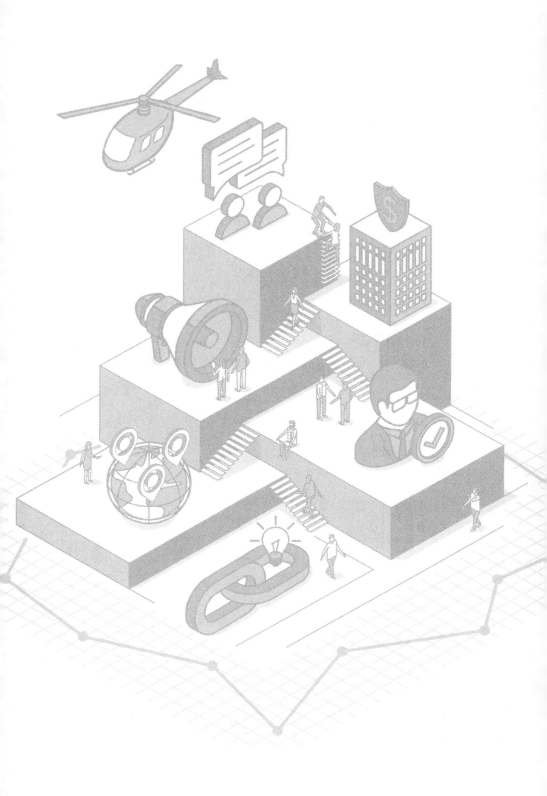

CHAPTER EIGHT

STRATEGY AND VISION COUNCIL

EXIT

BOARD

WORKING CAPITAL

CENTRAL BANK

GLOBAL LICENSING

EXPONENTIAL MARKETING

TALENT SYSTEM

INNOVATION PROCESS

ORGANIZATIONAL MODEL

One question that often arises when I tell people about the NOMEG model is, How is it possible to govern a company that's comprised of so many entrepreneurs, so many leaders? With such an abundance of creative and independent minds inside one company, it seems like a nightmare to manage it, right? But the nightmare gets corrected when you have a smart group of futurists and artists (in their own way) thinking about the challenges and opportunities a decade or more down the road.

That smart group of people is what I call the **strategy and vision council**, otherwise known as an advisory board or simply *the board*. This group of leaders meets quarterly to advise and make strategic decisions with the company leaders on a variety of issues facing the organization. The ultimate goal of the council or advisory board is to direct the future of the organization by planning and/or evaluating a ten-year or longer vision for where the organization should go.

Most people think of an advisory board as something that only very large, publicly traded companies have, but the NOMEG model demands that you rethink that idea. A NOMEG organization is comprised of so many leaders, which can give the impression that no one is really in charge of them. And if no one is in charge of them, then who is actually taking care of the organization? Remember that the CEO is in charge of the future, and the chief operating officer is only in charge of fixing operational problems. If those two executives are free to do as they wish, whom are they reporting to? They're reporting to the actual advisory board, or the council.

We've spoken a lot about what happens inside a NOMEG company from a short-term perspective, but there must be a point where someone is thinking about where the organization is heading in the next decade and beyond. I'm not referring to planning strategies from quarter to quarter or even solving a specific operational issue but rather the questions of where the organization is going and why, how long it will take to get there, and how it will reach this destination. That's where the strategy and vision council (aka an advisory board) come into play, existing as a group of experienced business and thought leaders who help guide the organization's long-term growth strategy.

The advisory board inhabits four stages, evolving from one to the other over a certain period of time as the organization grows: **operating**; **strategic**; **strategic and administrative**; and finally **strategic, administrative, and legal**.

Road Map for the Advisory Board

First of all, you need to have an advisory board from the company's inception. When you get your first leader, that's when you need to have a board. You don't need to wait until you reach a certain scale or generate a specific amount of annual revenue. That's a mistake. You need to have a strategy and vision council from the moment you onboard your first leader. This is something very different from traditional business models, which tell you not to worry about a board until you are much, much larger. But the board is actually a fairly early step to take in the NOMEG model, so let's examine what this board looks like and how it functions, starting with the basics.

Regardless of what you want to call it—an advisory board, a strategy and vision council, the Knights of the Round Table, the Jedi Council—it is usually comprised of an odd number, such as five, seven, or nine members. Each member serves a maximum of two years in their position. Obviously, we incorporate the owners of the company, and then you need to have a couple of external members on the board, meaning people who do not work within the organization. Generally speaking, you want those external members of the board to be your mentors or at least people you admire. You also want them to be people who are further down the empire-building road than you are. Their experience and expertise are what really change the face of the company. Having board members experienced in the entrepreneurial journey, who have the luxury of residing at a vantage point further away from the business, will help you think about new things on a quarterly basis, allowing for real change and difference for you and everyone else more intimately involved in the company.

When you're starting a company, no one really understands the seriousness of a board's purpose. I realized that early on in my own companies, so for the second advisory board meeting, we invited the leaders to present on their business units to the board. I still remember this meeting vividly because one of the leaders came in and said, "Members of the board, I really believe we need to invest in a drinking machine." He was talking about one of those water-purification machines for the office. "Because it's ridiculous. People don't have any water, and we need to have drinking water in the office." The room sat silent for a few awkward seconds as the board members looked around the table at one another. Finally, one of them said to me, "What the fuck is this guy talking about? This is a board meeting. Get the purified water machine, and get this [topic] out of the meeting."

From that experience and others, I understood clearly that people don't always know what a board is for, often thinking it's an opportunity to ask the company for stuff. The problem is that the board members are there to brainstorm strategies and solutions for future growth and innovation. Plus, these are valuable people, and you're paying them to be there.

Once I began doing a lot of mentoring, I realized that the operating board represents a stage wherein you need to ensure that your leaders understand that the board meeting is where they present their quarterly results and are afforded the opportunity to speak a little bit about their operational issues. They must know that the important part of the board is not just helping them solve operational problems but also giving them new ideas about how to improve their business results.

Usually, these meetings take about a half a day to a full day of work and they are conducted every quarter. The main structure of the meetings in the first stage, **operating**, is, again, for leaders to present their results for the quarter as well as their growth projections for the next year. This first stage of the advisory board is primarily designed to bring accountability to the leaders. These are the meetings we discussed in chapter 1 in which leaders are given three strikes to meet their goals. That's incredibly important for creating a sense of structure and accountability for the leaders, but it's also important for developing the mentoring of your leaders. In other words, the operating stage of the advisory board is designed to make accountability real for leaders, recognize them, and let them know that they're not alone as they work to grow their business unit.

Typically, you may spend one full year to transition from one stage to the next. That is not an exact rule, but it usually takes a couple meetings before your leaders familiarize themselves with the structure and purpose of each stage. Everyone will need time to evolve, so don't expect to walk into an advisory board and be in the fourth stage.

Once the unit leaders assimilate to this structure and the successful ones begin improving their numbers and rising to the top, evolution to the **strategic** stage of the advisory board will occur. This is the second of the four advisory board stages, wherein leaders understand that the main value of having an advisory board is obtaining new ideas for growth. You are still providing mentorship to the operational leaders, but now the board meetings are used primarily to outline strategic growth plans.

The main value of having an advisory board is obtaining new ideas for growth.

A year or so later, you should be ready to move into the third stage, the **strategic and administrative** stage. The only difference between this third stage and the second stage (strategic only) is that you will be giving the board the tools, the opportunity, and a little bit of the rope so they can change the financial structure of capital.

What does that mean? It means that if the advisory board believes that you're growing well in one business, they might ask for a round of debt financing (private debt), they might invite other investors, or they might even ask for a bank loan. They're going to change the financial structure of the company because they want to drive more growth.

To recap, the first stage is about solving operational problems and helping leaders get the results they need to stay in their position. Once you know they have these fundamentals down, you move on to the second stage, which is an advisory board that's helping you and the leaders with strategic ideas for growth. A third-stage council not only gives you ideas for growth but actually thinks about the fuel you're going to need money-wise to get there. They will also try to give recommendations on the capital and investment structures required to grow even faster.

For example, you might tell a leader, "Okay, you're growing so quickly. Why don't we get around to the financing specifically so that you can go into that market faster or so you can expand more quickly." In one of my recent board meetings, for instance, we did a round of debt specifically because we needed new software to improve a market study. So we borrowed money from the bank and did a small round of private debt, all based on the advice acquired during this board meeting.

The fourth stage is the **strategic, administrative, and legal stage**. As its name suggests, the only difference here is that you are including legal advisors in the meetings. This stage is necessary only if investors control a large stake in the company. Once that happens, they're going to ask to have seats on the board because they're putting a lot of money into the business and, therefore, will want a say in the decision-making. The only difference between the third and fourth stages is that the fourth stage gives seats specifically to people who have invested in the company but might not necessarily be part of the operating structure of the NOMEG model.

Organizing the Advisory Board

It's important to note that the board operates democratically, so every seat on the board is a vote. That's why you have to have odd numbers of five, seven, or nine. That's also why every seat is important. I wouldn't recommend having a board larger than nine people, because it slows down. We've tried it before, and the result was so many people talking that we couldn't move the needle forward on anything. You need agility, which a smaller board can provide. Bear in mind that you're looking for clarity in these meetings. If you don't get clarity, it's going to slow down your growth rather than accelerate it.

Keep in mind that the board has six primary purposes:

1. enforcing accountability;

2. providing guidance for leaders;

3. making key financial decisions;

4. defining massive transformative purpose (i.e., the "big, hairy, audacious goal");

5. branding; and

6. social activism.

Besides the actual operating plans, something else that's in the hands of the board comes from Jim Collins and Jerry Porras's book *Built to Last: Successful Habits of Visionary Companies*—the **big, hairy, audacious goal**, or *BHAG* for short. The BHAG is basically your ten-year goal for what the company wants to accomplish most of all, which is the primary focus of the advisory board. This is sort of your ideal goal that's essentially an attainable fantasy of where you want to take the company.

The board is in charge of the company's brand, so they can make recommendations specifically to the leaders in terms of safeguarding the value of the brand. For the NOMEG model to work best, it's very important to understand how you can create a chain of businesses and how to connect them. The company's brand is what connects all the businesses in that chain. In chapter one, we talked about business chains (i.e., business units linked together to feed one another) and how you don't want "a grocery store, a computer repair shop, and a nail salon" linked together because they are not links in the same chain but rather three different chains entirely. You want your chain of businesses to make sense on a brand level, and the board uses a panorama view to decide what the brand and, therefore, the business chains should be.

The board can even suggest a new business or experiment to the CEO. Likewise, they can also ask to kill off a business or to sell off one of the business units that isn't aligned with the direction of the brand. The board members are looking at the big picture and using a democratic approach to work together to scout the terrain for opportunities for both the company's brand and its ten-year-plus BHAG.

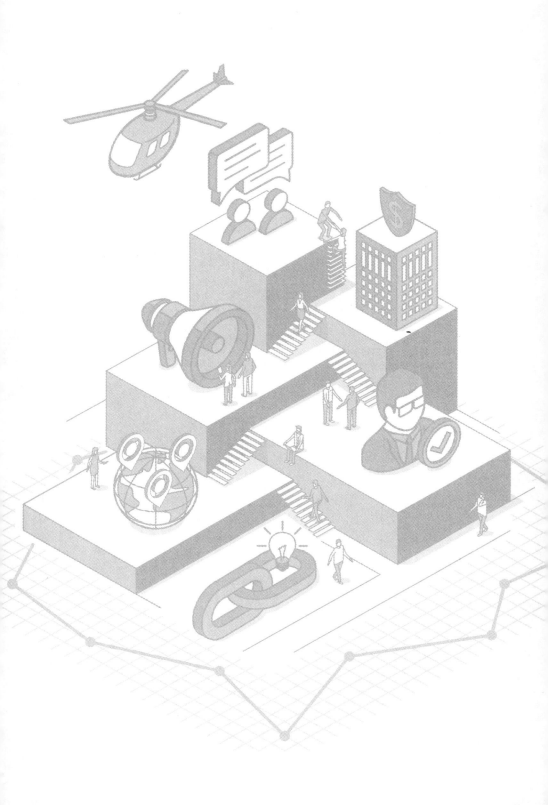

CHAPTER NINE

EXIT PATH

Managing NOMEG and Growth

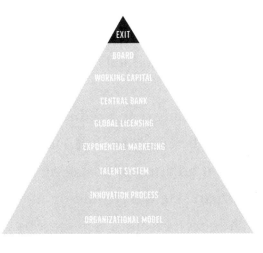

The decision to replace myself as CEO of my real estate consultancy, 4S Group, was an unexpected one on my part. The NOMEG model was working beautifully, and our business was growing rapidly, but I hadn't put much thought into my own trajectory beyond being the CEO. It was my company, and the CEO was the top position, so it seemed obvious that I would stay in that role until I either sold my share of the business and retired or died. But the old-school business ways were still clinging to my mind, and I didn't even know it until my business partner and COO at the time, Nacho, walked into my office one day with a bizarre proposition.

"I'm bored with my job," he told me. He said it so matter of factly and with such sureness that he might as well have been telling me the results of a blood test. Surprised and confused, I stared at him for a moment wondering whether he was joking. He assured me that he wasn't. "You can't be bored with that job," I told him. "There's no other job left that I can give you."

Nacho grinned and nodded his head. "Yes, there is. It's your job."

I was caught off guard and didn't immediately understand what I was listening to, but I trusted Nacho and knew this was not an attempt at staging a coup or hostile takeover on his part. He was reminding me that the model had reached the next level and a step must be taken to allow it to keep doing what it was designed to do: expand, evolve, innovate, and adapt to the needs of change, all to improve the company in every way possible.

I took some time to think about it, and within a day or so, I concluded that I would step aside and appoint Nacho as the new CEO. I was looking for four things in a CEO: **ability**, **likeability**, **teachability**, and **drive**. Those four traits are still mandatory for me when deciding to set someone onto the CEO course. I also knew that the best candidate to upskill to the role of CEO was the COO, and Nacho had proven himself time and again to be an excellent COO. Even though he would do things a little differently than I would do them as a CEO, I knew that he would be the best match for the company as CEO. That just left my own career's future to figure out, something I had not so much as wondered about since I'd started 4S Group. I had never pictured myself working outside my own company, and I had no idea how, or even *if*, I could.

In hindsight, I'm not sure whether I would have accepted Nacho's proposal had the circumstances been different. Purposefully or not, he chose the perfect time to pitch the idea to me. Deep down I had known for several months that it was time for me to move on and let the model play out the way it had been intended. I was also exhausted. I had been traveling almost nonstop for several years to research new ideas, secure new business, put out fires where needed, and more. I suspect that part of that busyness was my way of coping with the loss of my daughter. I had reached a point in which I was just too tired to keep juggling all my responsibilities as CEO, while also grieving and trying to be a supporting presence for my wife and family. Long before

I had never pictured myself working outside my own company, and I had no idea how, or even *if*, I could.

I admitted it, I was ready to take a step back and pursue a different direction.

Keep in mind that the CEO's main job in the NOMEG model is to create and execute innovations to help the company grow. My creativity was suffering under the weight of my schedule, and I realized that my physical exhaustion, grief, and growing responsibilities were making it impossible for me to be the kind of NOMEG CEO my company needed me to be. Creativity demands time and mental space to hallucinate, imagine, and look beyond the basic reality immediately before you. It's hard to create with a tangled mind. So I called Nacho and told him about my decision. Afterward, we sat down at a drawing board and sketched out a plan for my exit, which would ultimately take one year for me to leave the company as CEO. I would remain involved as a member of the board. As a board member, I would attend our board meetings every quarter to advise on ways to resolve internal problems, innovate business solutions and opportunities, and continue to scale the company and NOMEG model.

People often believe that when you exit your company, you get a big check and spend the rest of your days lying on a beachside hammock sucking down drinks brimming with flowers and fruit. It's not like that, at least not for most people and certainly not for me. You have to plan your exit very carefully, especially when no one is buying your company or your shares or if you aren't taking a huge severance payout. You have to plan a smooth transition not only for your exit but also for your successor's entrance, which often requires a period of consulting even after you exit.

The first step Nacho and I took was to let the central bank and the HR department know that they would be reporting to Nacho moving forward. Then, progressively, we created several different milestones in which I would hand over control of the company to him. Metaphorically speaking, rather than jumping off a speeding horse and letting him try to jump on, I would slow it down, help him up, and then hand him the reins one at a time before dismounting. After the transition was complete, we agreed that I would stay around as a consultant for three months to make sure there were no emergencies or doubts that might eventually stop the company in its tracks. We also decided that no CEO under the NOMEG model would get equity in the company right away. Rather, they would get a sliding scale of equity over a minimum of three years, depending on whether they could meet growth goals.

At the end of those three months, I came into the office for my last day, half expecting a surprise party for me, some kind of sentimental send-off celebration with lots of food and drinks and music, tearful speeches, and roaring laughter. Instead, it felt more like one of those clichéd movie scenes where a laid-off employee quietly packs their desk into a box and shuffles down the hallway and out the front door. Someone had grabbed some breakfast tacos on their way into work, and before they had all been scarfed down, Nacho told everyone to tell me good-bye because it was my last day.

My departure from the office was so comically unceremonious that it actually made my leaving easier, as it felt less final. And, of course, I wasn't really severing all ties with the company. I would still serve on the board to help make major decisions, and the executive team could always count on me to assist with any serious issues when needed. I would also still collect my cut of the revenue every month, which I had somewhat doubted would actually keep rolling in after the first quarter. Thankfully, everything worked perfectly, leading to my realization that my fear had been undermining my ability to exit the company all along.

I had a year to figure out what I was going to do next. It took me six months to determine what I wanted to do and another six months to bring that idea into existence. I had long wanted to create my real estate fund, so I spent six months creating the content that would eventually lead to my next companies: i11 Digital, an educational agency focused on real estate, entrepreneurship, and technology; and a financial company.

When I exited 4S, I took eight people with me to help launch whatever my next company would be. That team and I immersed ourselves in building our new endeavor over the next six months, during which time we gave ourselves complete freedom to explore our imaginations and experiment. It was one of the most fulfilling and exhilarating times of my professional life. I was charting the unknown with a young and ambitious crew of aspiring entrepreneurs and artists, only this time with the kind of experience, cash, and contacts that I could have only dreamed about when I began building 4S Group all those years before as a graduate student.

At i11 Digital, I got to see what a fully realized NOMEG model could do for a start-up. I got to watch it build an organizational structure from scratch and scale itself up in a way that I had not seen with 4S Group. There was little to no tweaking or testing required now that I had the formula down and knew that the model would work perfectly as long as I didn't get in its way. I realized, too, that the true beauty of the NOMEG model is that it actually breaks the glass ceilings that conventional models create for employees, allowing them to grow and ascend to whatever heights they wish. Clearly, 4S Group and Nacho were proof of that, since I had essentially fired myself and given the CEO position to one of my former employees. The model is capable of running itself. If you are smart enough to allow it, NOMEG can shed whatever was depleted in or harmful to the company to allow for new growth, almost as if it were a living organism itself.

If you come into a NOMEG company and do an extraordinary job, you can excel not only in your specific career path but also in multiple directions. Many people decide to change paths after college or after a few years spent doing the work they trained for. It's increasingly common for people to pivot and end up building a career doing something they never thought they would do. The NOMEG model offers the flexibility to make those kinds of changes. If you excel at your job within a NOMEG company, you can become a business unit leader, which puts you on a direct track to one day being the COO, CMO, or CEO of the company. Or you can choose the path of a regional partner, which positions you to be the owner and leader of your own company if you should choose. In the simplest of terms, you can either position yourself to be a high-level leader within someone else's company or you can gain the connections, knowledge, and experience to build your own large business. The NOMEG model creates a path for someone to start literally with zero and build themselves up from there in multiple directions.

As an owner of a NOMEG company, you will eventually have to give up some equity in the company in order to let its growth pattern continue. However, you are only giving up equity to people who you know are specifically qualified to earn that equity, people who you know will take the company to a new level. These are not people you hire for the job externally, meaning you hire another company's CEO to take over your job. You are promoting someone from within your company, who you know has won that job by proving their merit over and over again in NOMEG's intense system of education and testing. At that point, you will serve as a consultant, board member, or simply as a shareholder who does nothing but collect their share of the company's earnings each week, month, quarter, year, etc. To use sports as an analogy, you are essentially stepping down as the star player or head coach of your team and moving to the role of general manager, athletic director, or just an owner who is largely uninvolved in the day-to-day operations of the team.

I'm often asked how soon you can exit one of your companies under the NOMEG model. Obviously, that depends on a multitude of factors, including the area of business, the market economy, the company's organization, etc. In general, though, six years is the minimum amount of time you should expect to lead the company as CEO before you can begin easing your way out of the position. I started i11 Digital in January 2019, and I've already set a path to exit the company by 2025.

After I exited 4S Group, I came to appreciate the exit strategy in a completely different way. Before my departure from 4S Group, I had a fear of exiting. Subconsciously—and because traditional business books and "experts" teach us to be this way—I retained some belief that my company would implode on itself or that competitors would defeat it. Given what we have been taught about business and business leadership, that's an understandable fear. After leaving my company and starting another, I realized that having an exit path is the only way to overcome that fear. That realization led to a greater appreciation for a model like NOMEG, which allows a company to move on its own, inevitably creating structures that make a leader's exit easier and less disruptive to the company as a whole.

I also saw the need to create the "next big thing," not only small things. It's necessary to build small things in your company, like individual business units, but you also need to be able to step back and create big ideas that you're willing and able to execute. When the timing is right, you must be able to walk away from everything you've built and begin the process of creating something big all over again.

As CEO, that is part of your job. Remember that the CEO is in charge of creating the talent machine, handling acquisitions, overseeing the central bank, and spurring business innovations. Planning out an exit path for yourself is part of your responsibilities under the umbrella of business innovations. Perhaps the most difficult part of creating an exit path in the NOMEG model is that it requires the CEO to train the right person within the company over a period of time, often years, to take over the position. That's the real challenge: building up the knowledge, patience, and time to upskill someone who is capable of sliding into the role of CEO without creating too many waves in the wake of your departure.

You take someone early on in the talent machine who is aspiring to be a business unit leader, and if they do well, you might give them more units or make them a regional partner, depending on their goals. Eventually, you might promote them to CMO or COO and then upskill them from that position to the role of CEO, which will require them to think further outside the box and have a complete understanding of not only how the NOMEG model works but also why it's so effective and why not even the CEO role is bigger than the model. A CEO trainee must understand the technical nature of the job, but they also need to have the ability to see what the next challenges will be and what skills they will need to master, not just for the job they're currently in but also for their next job and the one after that. They must have vision, and they must know how to prepare themselves for each stage of that vision.

The work of transitioning to CEO is not solely on the trainee's shoulders. The company needs to make time for mentorship, during which time the current CEO can teach their trainee the skills, responsibilities, strategies, and general information they'll need to be a successful predecessor. Even if the trainee was upskilled from intern to business unit leader to regional partner to COO, training them for the CEO position can still take a year or longer to complete. During that time, you will also need to find a replacement for whatever position they're vacating. Prior to Nacho's official appointment as 4S Group's new CEO, for example, we brought in one of our regional partners to train under Nacho for the COO role.

It's important to note that someone new to the leadership team (e.g., COO, CMO, CFO, etc.) does not immediately receive equity in the company. There should be a contract in place outlining a multiyear plan in which a specific set of goals must be met before the new leader can receive equity. They will be compensated the same amount as their previous position, but they will get phantom stocks in the company. At the end of their trial period, usually three years, they will receive real stock in the company or a percentage of the company's total profits. This three-year trial period is about more than seeing whether they can perform the general duties of their new role; you also want to see whether they can *improve* the company through their new role.

A leader's ability to reach or exceed agreed-upon milestones, such as growth goals, is obviously an easy way to determine whether they are in the proper role, but you want to look at how strong their soft skills are as well. Communication, teamwork, problem solving, adaptability, conflict resolution, dependability, work ethic, receptiveness to criticism, and general emotional intelligence are all examples of soft skills. As you may already know, they are some of the hardest skills for people to learn. That's why we bring all aspiring leaders into a practice we call ***un lugar en la mesa***, which means "a place at the table." As the name suggests, current leaders bring in leadership candidates to group mentorships and collective intelligence sessions to help teach them soft skills through a number of exercises in which the candidate practices their response to various scenarios they will likely encounter in the respective role they want to fill. Remember that the NOMEG model *creates* leaders. We do not go out and try to find them in the talent market; we want to build them ourselves so they can run NOMEG companies the way they're intended to operate. That's why it's so important to have formal procedures in place for how the leadership table works.

The leadership table is very interesting because it actually breaks down hierarchies. The leadership table is a place that anyone in the company can reach, where they will be upskilled for bigger roles by mentors with the skills and experience the candidate will need to be successful. Regardless of the job-specific skills they will need, I generally look for four things in any leadership candidate as I work to grow them: **ability**, **likeability**, **teachability**, and **drive**.

Obviously, they need to have the technical abilities that the job demands. You wouldn't hire an accountant who has no understanding of numbers, just as you shouldn't promote someone to CMO if they have no knowledge of marketing whatsoever. That's an easy one. Likeability, on the other hand, is a skill that's a bit trickier to assess and even harder to teach. I judge a person's likeability not by whether I personally like them but rather by how well they can manage people. Do they communicate well with others? Do the people they're managing listen to them? Do they respect them? Are they able to resolve conflicts quickly and productively? Are they open to feedback, even when it's negative? These types of questions all reveal features of a person's overall likeability from a leadership perspective.

Teachability is not just about how much information a candidate's able to absorb, understand, and recall but how open someone is to being coached as well. That's why teachability and drive go hand in hand; if a person doesn't want to learn new things, then they don't have the drive that's needed to take on new responsibilities, much less be a leader who's capable of constant innovation and growth.

Transitioning leaders in and out of roles is a relay race, only with several batons being passed between several people simultaneously. Make sure you give yourself enough time to guarantee that those handoffs go as smoothly as possible. More importantly, take the time to carefully observe each new leader's performance over a number of years to ensure that you aren't giving up equity in your company to the wrong people.

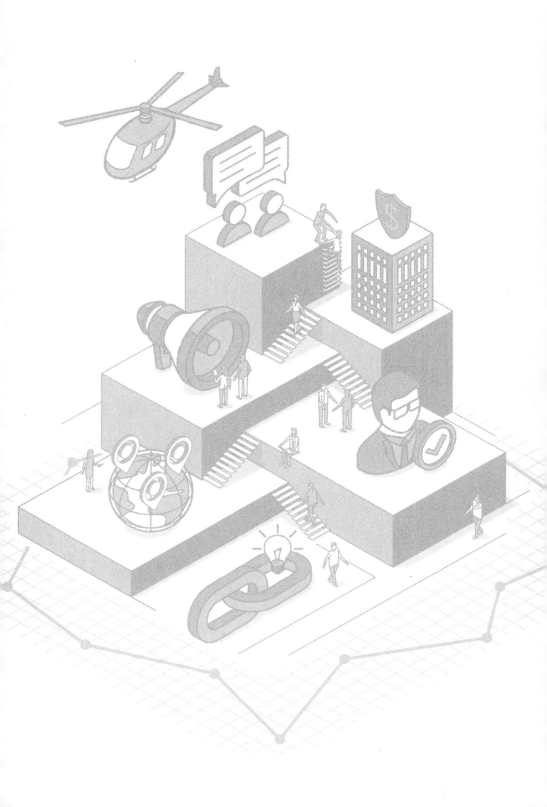

BETA MODE

It may be your goal to achieve success in business for yourself, but once you do, your primary goal shifts to maintaining that success. Anyone who has been able to build a successful business knows that keeping it going can be even more challenging than building it in the first place. We know that if we're not trying to learn something new and execute innovative ways to continue growing, we are failing the organizations we lead. To be successful at that portion of leadership, in part, requires a nature of curiosity. If you are curious, then you'll want to find out what else is out there. You'll have an unquenchable thirst to look around the next corner of the journey and see what may lie ahead. For me, I also know that if I don't bring the rest of my team on that learning journey with me, I am failing both them and myself.

There are two types of mindsets among leaders—and people in general: those with a **fixed mindset** and those with a **growth mindset**. The terms are pretty self-explanatory. Those who don't want to learn and evolve have a fixed mindset, which is terrible for growth. They cripple not only the leader's power to invoke progress but also the entire organization's opportunities for finding a better way. It doesn't mean growth can't occur; a single engine can still propel a plane forward. But it will be harder to control as the organization expands. When organizations grow, their focus often broadens. Your consumer base, client and member profile, staff, policies, and the markets that impact them all widen and change as a result of outstanding growth. Eventually, though, that single-engine mentality will only propel the organization into a tailspin.

The number one predictor of an impending tailspin of this type is if the leaders project an unbridled ego. A healthy ego is important for leaders at every level, of course. They need confidence to lead others and execute difficult tasks. It's when egos get out of check and cultures celebrate a hero-worship view of leaders that the fixed mindset emerges. Few people readily acknowledge they have a fixed mindset, but many leaders who have been successful, particularly when they've had few failures in their history, increasingly believe they have the answers and fail to listen and learn. Bringing humility back to every level of an organization is one of the most critical needs in today's fast-paced, competition-everywhere business landscape.

People who make it to the top of an organization often rely too much on themselves. They view themselves as the boss and believe that whatever they think and say should be written in stone, even when the weight of such a mentality becomes too heavy and the mistakes begin to pile up. A fixed mindset inherently becomes narrower with growth, rendering one's once-great ability to solve problems and fuel growth incredibly limited. As it's been said many times, two heads are better than one. Why not take advantage of that fact? You have more to gain than you have to lose when so much is on the line.

A growth mindset, as I'm sure you've guessed, refers to the ability to predict, plan, adapt, and innovate for the future. The success of all those characteristics relies on cohesion within the organization, a pivotal component of all great companies. You might say that a team that learns together stays together. When leaders foster an environment of learning, they enable their team to take an active part in the organization's development. By allowing everyone, from the bottom to the top, to contribute new ideas, strategies, and tools, you're providing more chances for a problem to get solved. Perhaps even more importantly, by listening and leading with questions instead of answers, leaders can spot new opportunities more readily. Leaders need to be examples of growth by constantly learning and sharing with their team what they have learned. And while it may not be possible to give a fair testing period to everyone's ideas, a leader who is receptive to the input of others creates an atmosphere that encourages people to contribute as much as they can to their work.

There are a few tips I'd like to leave you with to help you keep your growth mindset on track, especially as your business begins to expand. The first is to listen and ask questions before sharing your opinion. Oftentimes a person taking the risk to present a new and contrary viewpoint or idea is shut down because one or more people in the room quickly shoot holes in it. That results in the best idea losing out to the idea(s) of the most stubborn and often most fixed-minded people in the room. The key here is truly listening before asking any clarifying questions. Don't spend time thinking about what you're going to say in response to someone when they speak. Instead, use the time to hear what they have to say and formulate your questions. After you've had this exchange of questions and answers, it's fine to share your views, but this extra "oxygen" being thrown into the process allows a fledgling idea to have at least a chance of taking hold in a discussion.

First is to listen and ask questions before sharing your opinion.

The second tool to keep a growth mindset sharp is to encourage **debate**. The goal behind this tactic is to get everyone in the room to listen and consider new ideas fully. After the Q&A is complete, each person in the room is required to argue both *for* and *against* the new idea. By requiring everyone to debate both sides of the topic, they have to expend intellectual and emotional capacity to really think through the ideas. It's amazing how often you'll find people switching their views as you go through this exercise.

What's Next?

By now, you have finally built, or are at least prepared to build, the complete pyramid of the NOMEG model. If you have already implemented this book in your own business, congratulations. I'm certain that there is a completely different and more successful road ahead for you. I do, however, want to add some words of warning for the method. We are living in a world that is faster and more connected than anyone could have dreamed of even twenty years ago, so the model you have read about in this book was actually planned for 2022.

We put this version of NOMEG through an extreme testing period during the COVID-19 pandemic of 2020–2021, which obviously stretched or broke a lot of business models around the world. Through the many trials and obstacles of the pandemic, however, we realized that the NOMEG model was strong enough to sustain and even support our businesses and partners during the most globally impactful crisis of our generation. There were a few key components of NOMEG that I believe enabled us to adapt and endure the enormous challenges brought on by the pandemic. One was the variable pay structure used in the NOMEG model, which creates a very lightweight company. Because a company is lightweight in terms of its pay structure, you can easily maneuver throughout periods of time when the income is not that great.

NOMEG also enables much greater speeds of innovation, which allowed us to iterate several different digital business models. Because of the size of teams within the NOMEG model and the speeds at which those teams can work, we were able to move much quicker into a digital offering of our goods and services.

I am sure that, as time passes, some concepts of the model presented in this book will have to evolve and other concepts may even have to perish entirely. But the important thing to understand is that NOMEG is, in essence, an operating system in **beta mode**, a term used in software development for software that is not yet fully complete. That's exactly how we should look at this version of NOMEG.

We do not believe that this is a finished model. We believe that this is an eternal work in progress. What that means is that as you start to use the principles in this book inside your mind as you structure companies, you're going to have to add processes at times. You will have to fill in the blanks, so to speak, as technologies and the societies using those technologies change and evolve. Remember that this book is not meant to be the complete and only book on this model. Rather, it's meant to be the beta version of a new organization-focused operating system.

Throughout the coming years, I will be updating the materials on a digital platform that you have here: http://nomeginstitute.com/. In other words, this is a conversation that will continue in digital form as the world in which we live—and thus the NOMEG model itself—evolves in real time. For that reason, this is not the end of the book, but rather it is only the beginning of an ongoing, adaptive journey toward customizing and implementing the NOMEG model for your specific business and life as time marches on.

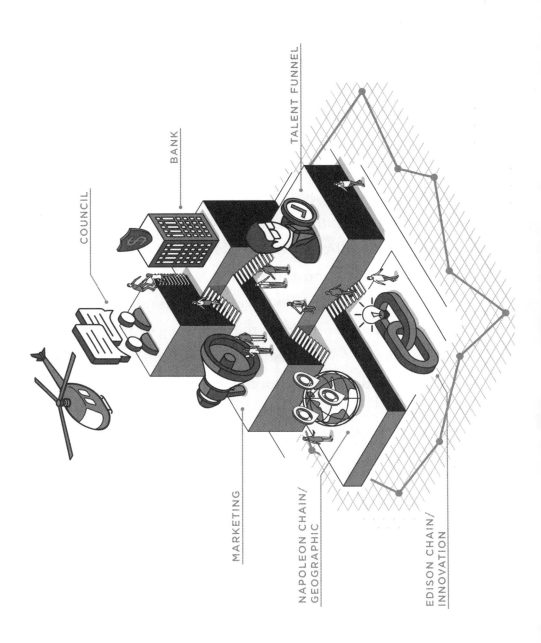

COUNCIL

BANK

TALENT FUNNEL

MARKETING

NAPOLEON CHAIN/
GEOGRAPHIC

EDISON CHAIN/
INNOVATION

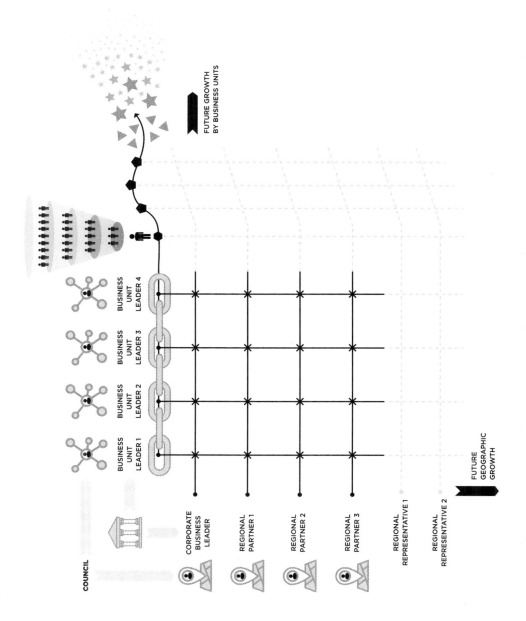

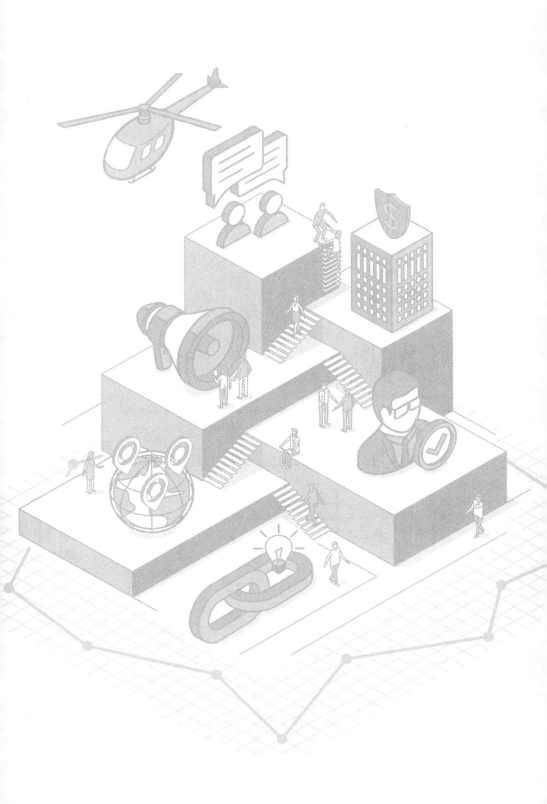

NOTES